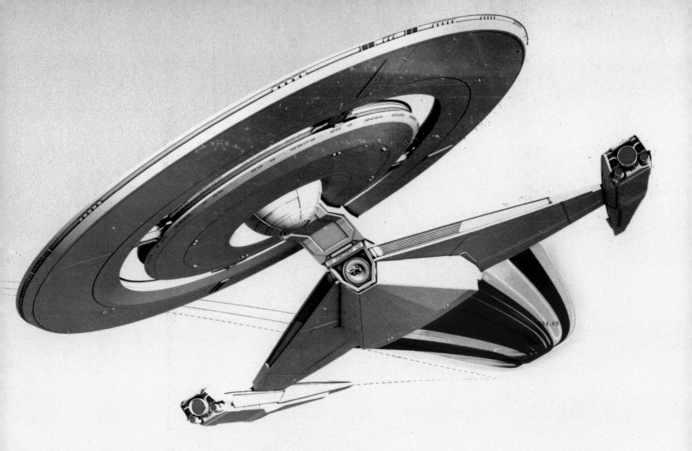

THE STORY OF
STAR TREK: DISCOVERY

The first new series of *Star Trek* in a dozen years, *Star Trek: Discovery* Season 1 tells a story quite unlike any of its franchise forebears. Though set 10 years prior to the original series, it's a supremely modern *Star Trek* for the streaming age – a serialized "novel" comprising 15 thrilling chapters, packed with twists and turns.

But the story of Season 1 is more than just the tale of the *U.S.S. Discovery* and her crew – of Michael Burnham, Gabriel Lorca, Saru, Paul Stamets, Sylvia Tilly, Ash Tyler, and all the other characters whose lives are delineated across 15 exhilarating episodes. It's also the story of a gigantic creative collaboration – of how hundreds of actors, producers, writers, designers, costumers, make-up artists, and visual effects creators brought *Star Trek* back to the small screen.

In this companion to *Discovery* Season 1, that story is told by some of those people – episode by episode, in the words of those who know it best.

TITAN EDITORIAL
Editor Nick Jones
Senior Editor Martin Eden
Assistant Editor Jake Devine
Senior Production Controller
Jackie Flook
Production Supervisor
Maria Pearson
Production Controller
Peter James
Art Director Oz Browne
Sales & Circulation Manager
Steve Tothill

Subscriptions Executive
Tony Ho
Direct Sales & Marketing Manager
Ricky Claydon
Commercial Manager
Michelle Fairlamb
Designer Dan Bura
U.S. Advertising Manager Jeni Smith
Publishing Manager Darryl Tothill
Publishing Director Chris Teather
Operations Director Leigh Baulch
Executive Director Vivian Cheung
Publisher Nick Landau

CONTRIBUTORS
Bryan Cairns
Natalie Clubb
Christopher Cooper
Marian Cordry
Pat Jankiewicz
Joe Nazzaro
Jay Stobie

DISTRIBUTION
US Newsstand: Total Publisher Services, Inc.
John Dziewiatkowski, 630-851-7683
US Distribution: Source Interlink, Curtis Circulation
Company
UK Newsstand: Marketforce, 0203 7879199
US/UK Direct Sales Market: Diamond Comic
Distributors
For more info on advertising contact
adinfo@titanemail.com

Star Trek: Discovery The Official Companion is
published by Titan Magazines, a division of Titan
Publishing Group Limited, 144 Southwark Street,
London SE1 0UP. For sale in the US, Canada,
UK and Eire
ISBN: 9781785861918

Printed in the U.S. by Quad.

CONTENTS

FEATURES

EPISODE GUIDE

MAKING
DISCOVERY

EIGHT KEY BEHIND-THE-SCENES PLAYERS
OUTLINE THE CREATIVE PROCESSES – AND
ACCOMPANYING CHALLENGES – INVOLVED
WITH BRINGING THIS BOLD NEW SERIES
OF *STAR TREK* TO THE SMALL SCREEN.

GRETCHEN J. BERG

EXECUTIVE PRODUCER/SHOWRUNNER

"We usually start [in the *Star Trek: Discovery* writers' room] where we ended the night before – with character arcs and particular story beats. It's a giant brainstorming session that ends when people say, 'Okay, we realize the shape of that,' and we start writing these beats down and making it real by putting it up on the board.

"I came to *Star Trek* late in life, but we immediately understood what the future was supposed to look like. Collaboration helps; it's very easy to fall down a rabbit hole when writing by yourself, but I have a writing partner, [fellow showrunner] Aaron Harberts.

"The new show is in the same timeline as the original series. This is the Prime universe and we are pretty close to when the original series happens.

"We are aware it is a different era and a different format for the show. I don't think we were gunning for shock value. Everything always comes out of character and story. If it feels like something that would happen in that world and in that context, we go in that direction. It is not a group that leads with wanting to shock people or horrify people."

AARON HARBERTS

EXECUTIVE PRODUCER/SHOWRUNNER

"What Gretchen and I loved about this version of *Star Trek* was its serialization. There's a lot to track, just to monitor where the characters are and how the unifying theme of the season is working its way out. One entire wall of the whiteboard [in the writers' room] is dedicated to chapters in this novel and it's adjusting all the time. That's one wall. Another is just characters all the way down with episodes across the top. The theme of the first season was finding one's humanity and finding one's purpose.

"It's all about mapping. Before we do a lot of writing, we really have to do a lot of long-range planning. That's what we've been doing for Season 2.

"It's a beautiful opportunity that we have to write for *Star Trek*, because you can tackle so many issues in such interesting ways.

"[Season 1] was an interesting season because it was set against the backdrop of war. One of the things we are looking forward to in Season 2 is a tone that we can now be in a more exploratory phase and a more diplomatic phase – maybe a bit more of a *Trek*ian chapter. But everything for us is really driven by character.

"The idea was to always be in the Prime timeline. Obviously, there are questions and concerns and things that are different. Our technology is a little different – we have a ship that runs very differently. We are our own show in a lot of ways.

"We bump up against the *Enterprise* at the end of our finale and we know what kind of uniforms they wear, so we will leave it at that. Alex Kurtzman was very involved in the *Enterprise* redesign.

"As a gay man, what is really important to me about presenting gay characters is that they always lead with their competence and their character first, not with their sexuality. That is true of all of our characters on our bridge. All of our characters who are so different, they lead with their professionalism and their strong character first. So you may already have a window into a [gay] relationship and just don't know it."

TAMARA DEVERELL

PRODUCTION DESIGNER

"Gretchen and Aaron wanted the mycelial network to look like a particular succulent, the 'sticks on fire' [*Euphorbia tirucalli*], so that became the whole thing. We did some concept art and then VFX took it over for the interweaving. I did some of my own concept work for it, describing this strange, weird world that didn't really exist because we're shooting one actor twice against a green screen. There was no set involved, just conceptualizing.

"We reduce, reuse, and recycle! When we had to tear down the Sarcophagus ship, it was a very sad day. We actually did a ceremony with the entire art department in the ship... We kept parts of it because I knew we would reuse it again. One of the best parts was the floor – this beautiful, backlit elemented floor – and we stood it up as a wall in another set. We took all of the pieces, all a part of a beautiful Klingon world, and re-sculpted them on a very grand scale. They're fun easter eggs for viewers to see and find.

"For the *Enterprise*, we based it originally off of the original series. We were really drawing a lot of materials from that. And then we rejigged it a bit to particularly go more toward the *Star Trek* movies, which is a little bit fatter, a little bit bigger. Overall, I think we expanded the length of it to be within the world of *Discovery*, which is bigger, so we did cheat it as a larger ship.

"We build a lot of things, so we have a big art department; about 20 designers out here in LA, and a lot in Toronto."

04 Anthony Rapp as Lieutenant Paul Stamets, mycelial network expert.

05 Michael Burnham aboard the extraordinary Sarcophagus ship.

06 Burnham in her Mirror Universe Terran Empire uniform.

07 Shazad Latif, as the Klingon Voq, wields a deadly bat'leth.

GERSHA PHILLIPS

COSTUME DESIGNER

"I start [each episode] by gathering some research and some images I like that inspire or talk to the design I want to create. It's very collaborative between myself and the illustrator, Christian Cordella; I feel the design comes together from between the two of us, as opposed to being just my idea. We start to gather and work on it. He starts a first draft and then a second, depending on how far it evolves. There's a really cool dynamic between the two of us, tossing it back and forth, and developing it.

"I love to get it to a point where I can sell [the costume design] to Gretchen and Aaron, where they like it and are enthusiastic about it too. Each design has to evoke some kind of emotion.

"When we were coming up with concepts for the Mirror Universe, Tamara, the Production Designer, had the idea for brutalist architecture as a jumping-off point. I took that to my illustrator, as we were working on imagery. I took him a filigree of a pattern that I liked and I said, 'I need you to take this into a brutalist language.' That's the print you see on the chestplates. Tamara took that and reused it on the ship in different places. It started with Tamara, then to me and back to her, which is really cool."

> "I think the prop we had the most fun with in the first season was the Klingon bat'leth."
>
> **MARIO MOREIRA**

MARIO MOREIRA

PROPERTY MASTER

"For us, the process starts with the script, the story. We break down the scripts, find what we need for each episode, and then we talk to other departments and then our bosses, Tamara, and Gersha, because a lot of our stuff works together. Then we farm it out and decide what shop would be best for that build.

"We've got access to some of the best ship and prop makers in the world – because we happen to be *Star Trek* and it's helpful to be able to just call them and say, 'Hey, do you want to build something for *Star Trek*?'

"I think the prop we had the most fun with in the first season was the Klingon bat'leth. It's a real synthesis of materials, and getting it to the finish line with the redesign was such a marathon of collaboration. We had such nerdy discussions about what minerals were available on Qo'noS, and it got to the point where we were saying, 'We're getting paid to talk like this! It's so fun!'

"Eventually, it was a steel interior with an aluminum shaft. We cut in places and attached latex and rubber, then carved that out to give it that stone look. We used traditional 3D printing for the handles. It's my favorite prop.

"We're all into 3D printing technology on the show – it has revolutionized what we do. Take the phaser – we start out with sketches, then 3D model it. Previously, I would go to the workshop and start scraping something out of styrofoam until we had the right shape, then go to everybody and ask, 'How do you feel about this?' Now we just hit 'print' and by the weekend, we've all got it and can hold it in the shape we want. We adjusted the phaser grip a little bit and that was it. For very little money, you can go to town."

GLENN HETRICK

ALCHEMY STUDIOS/PROSTHETIC AND
SPECIAL FX MAKE-UP

"I remember freaking out the first time I saw the word 'Klingon' in the title of an email between Gretchen, Aaron, Neville [Page, creature designer], and myself. It was like an out-of-body experience.

"The 3D printing is great. Neville and I [at Alchemy FX] had the great fortune of working with 3D Systems as a partner, one of the leading 3D printing companies in the world. We thought, 'What better show to integrate that paradigm and explore how 3D printing technology can impact make-up FX design better than *Star Trek*?' It's a perfect marriage. When we approached the design of the Klingons, it's not just in our hard surfacing. The Torchbearer's helmet is actually a printed piece, while some of his suit is traditional foam latex but it's from a printed piece.

"Our approach to the Klingons' [look] is we loved it so much, we wanted it to resonate and make it more real than it's ever been. 3D printing allows us to create extremely complex shapes on the occipital lobe and the ridge on their necks. We printed those pictures, ran them in clay, and allowed the sculptors to use the hyper-detailed pieces and integrate them into the sculpt as they found the personality of each Klingon in each house. It's been an incredibly exciting process.

"We start with a keen eye turned toward canon. We start there always, which you can really see with The Andorians and Tellarites.

"The impetus [for the radical Klingon redesign] lies in the earliest conversations with the writers and producers… We were talking about what would the difference be, if you are going to take another [evolutionary] step. I am as much of a [*Star Trek*] fan as you guys, and when Neville and I stepped into that world, we knew that it could not be something completely different. You need to honor and maintain as much of the integrity of the concept of the Klingons.

"So what we did is started dissecting through the lens of the canon. What is their species? What is their DNA? It is sort of a cross between reptilian and avian. And once we struck upon that concept, as with all of our aliens, the evolutionary imperative drives our decision. Every single thing has to be for a reason. It can't just be because it looks cool. It needs to have a function, and form follows that.

"So that is how [the Klingon redesign] started. I am also not going to lie to you: both Neville and I are huge H. R. Giger fans, so that is the seasoning. If you look at it that way, you can see a lot of Giger-type designs that are sort of tertiary details on top of all the form and sub-form. There is still much to be seen and it is still an ongoing conversation. The Klingon Empire is vast… and there are so many things I want to tell you, but I can't!"

08

> "You need to honor and maintain as much of the integrity of the concept of the Klingons."
>
> **GLENN HETRICK**

08 Mary Chieffo as L'Rell – one of *Star Trek: Discovery*'s remarkable Klingons.

09 Jason Isaacs as Captain Lorca interacts with one of the show's more subtle visual effects.

10 Burnham makes a bloody discovery in "Context Is for Kings."

JASON ZIMMERMAN

VISUAL EFFECTS SUPERVISOR

"The organizational part of creating VFX is something that you set up at the beginning, and if everything runs well you don't have to think about it any more. So if you know that you need a *Discovery* ship, and you know somebody's gonna work on the *Discovery* ship, you let them get on with it and you don't have to worry about that part of it any more.

"It's all about the planning and picking your vendors wisely. Fortunately, I started as a compositor, as an artist, 20 years ago, and knowing what it's like on that side, and the organizational challenges of getting artists and all that stuff, kind of helps us. And the people that work with me have also been there as well, so they understand the challenges on their end when it comes to working on shots.

"We have good relationships with our vendors; it's various places that we've worked with before – Piximodo is one of the big ones. We have a relationship where we'll call them up and say, 'Hey, how do we do this?' It's like a family – they will work with us, they help us out, we help them out, we do the best that we can. Everybody cares ultimately about what it looks like, so we're always gonna get there.

"In addition to the amazing and glamorous shots of the ships, in visual FX these days, there's a lot of invisible FX in the show that you don't notice – whether it's adding blood or extending a set. There's times when we're called to add a hallway or extend a set to give the shot scope. That's what's fun for us; a full shot in space, you know that's CG visual FX, but sometimes ▶

11 A visual effects debris field on the *U.S.S. Discovery* main screen, in "Despite Yourself."

12 Visual effects and sets merge seamlessly on the Sarcophagus ship.

13 Kasseelian opera soundtracks the love between Hugh Culber (Wilson Cruz) and Paul Stamets.

14 Paul Stamets: smarter than the average scientist.

> "In addition to the amazing and glamorous shots of the ships, in visual FX these days, there's a lot of invisible FX in the show that you don't realize we did, whether it's adding blood or extending a set."
>
> **JASON ZIMMERMAN**

it's the shot where we removed something from the background or extended a hall and you don't know that was us until you see behind-the-scenes footage.

"When you build something digitally, it can't look CG – it has to look real, so it doesn't draw the eye away from the story. You have to add textures and things so it looks real, so the CG looks like it lives in the world.

"It starts with [the producers] giving us designs to work with and then there is a lot of back and forth between VFX and [Tamara's] department to make sure that we get everything right. There were a lot of conversations and more emails than I could remember about how the design would evolve and match our universe, and that is how we arrived where we are now."

JEFF RUSSO

COMPOSER

"I had never written anything for an operatic voice before, and when Aaron [Harberts] called me earlier in the season to tell me, 'We're gonna have an opera this season and I would love for you to write this,' I thought, 'Ohhh, great!'

"It was one of these things where you sit down and think… We have these two characters [Stamets and Culber], and the story is that one loved [Kasseelian opera] and the other didn't, but it still had to carry this emotional tone to it. I had to think about their backstory, and about their story going forward. At that point, when I started writing it, I had no idea yet what was going to happen, because I wasn't reading scripts anymore because I wanted to keep myself surprised – and boy, did that surprise me!

"Because of that, it really helped me feel what they were gonna feel. I brought in a spectacular singer, Iona, and we played around with some chord progressions, and I had her singing in the room with me until I stumbled onto something that I thought was really great. I ended up writing a lot more than we ended up using.

"I have a Spock doll that sits on my piano and I talk to him… Oddly enough, it helps!"

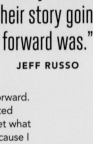

> "I had to think about Stamets and Culber's backstory, and what their story going forward was."
>
> **JEFF RUSSO**

13

14

THE VULCAN HELLO

SEASON 1, EPISODE 1

First aired:
September 24, 2017
Teleplay: Bryan Fuller &
Akiva Goldsman
Story: Bryan Fuller &
Alex Kurtzman
Director: David Semel

CAST

Sonequa Martin-Green:
Commander Michael
Burnham
Doug Jones: Lieutenant
Commander Saru
Michelle Yeoh: Captain
Philippa Georgiou
Mary Chieffo: L'Rell
James Frain: Sarek
Chris Obi: T'Kuvma
Maulik Pancholy:
Doctor Anton Nambue
Terry Serpico:
Admiral Brett Anderson
Sam Vartholomeos:
Ensign Danby Connor
Arista Arhin:
Young Michael Burnham
Emily Coutts:
Lieutenant Keyla Detmer
Justin Howell:
Torchbearer/Rejac
**Javid Iqbal (Shazad
Latif):** Voq
Ali Momen:
Lieutenant Kamran Gant
**David Benjamin
Tomlinson:** Or'Eq
Tasia Valenza:
Computer Voice
Chris Violette:
Lieutenant Britch Weeton
Romaine Waite:
Lieutenant Troy Januzzi

01

SYNOPSIS

Stardate 1207.3, Earth year 2256. Under the command of Captain Philippa Georgiou, the *U.S.S. Shenzhou* encounters a mysterious object in the depths of an impenetrable asteroid belt at the edge of Federation space. To investigate, the *Shenzhou*'s first officer, Commander Michael Burnham, suits up and heads out on an EVA.

Cut off from the ship, Burnham marvels at the object's ancient craftsmanship – before realizing the markings on its hull plating are Klingon. Suddenly, Burnham is confronted by a ritualistically armored Klingon warrior. When this "Torchbearer" attacks the commander, he is impaled on his own bat'leth and killed, with dire consequences not only for Burnham, but for galactic peace.

> "We come in peace, that's why we're here. Isn't that the whole idea of Starfleet?"
>
> **MICHAEL BURNHAM**

With a cloaked Klingon vessel sending out a mysterious signal, and a nearby Andorian colony possibly under threat, Georgiou attempts to follow Starfleet protocol and reason with the commander of the aggressive Klingon ship. However, Burnham – who has returned to the *Shenzhou* suffering from radiation sickness and concussion – has an alternative plan: to meet the Klingons on a level they will understand by opening fire. When Georgiou refuses to do so, the Vulcan-raised Burnham knocks her captain out using a nerve pinch and takes command of the ship.

But before the *Shenzhou* can fire a shot, a fleet of Klingon ships drops out of warp, leaving the lone Starfleet vessel heavily outnumbered – and outgunned…

> "Captain, we have to give the Klingons a Vulcan 'hello.'"
>
> MICHAEL BURNHAM

03 Georgiou and Burnham reactivate a dry well on the desert planet.

04 L'Rell reacts to T'Kuvma's rousing words.

AARON HARBERTS
Executive Producer

"Even though they aired in prime-time, those first two episodes – that's prologue. You'd never get a broadcast network to sign off on a prologue where Michelle Yeoh's character dies; that just wouldn't happen.

"Likability is a buzzword that you hear a lot in broadcast television; they want [characters] to be welcomed into [viewers'] homes right out of the gate. The freedom that we had, with the character of Michael Burnham, to start her in a very different place – that was a gift. And also we had the opportunity to do things like start with Mary's character, L'Rell – who was just a bridge officer on the Sarcophagus ship – and then take her to a place where suddenly she's ruling the Klingon Empire."

03

(Previous spread)

01 Captain Georgiou (Michelle Yeoh) and Commander Burnham (Sonequa Martin-Green) on a vital mission on a desert world.

02 L'Rell (Mary Chieffo) with T'Kuvma (Chris Obi).

04

MICHELLE YEOH
Captain Philippa Georgiou

"When Michael Burnham arrived, she was like a solid piece of ice. Captain Georgiou and Sarek don't want to break her spirit, as she's worked so hard to be who she is. But they want her to understand that there is more than that, that it is okay to have these good emotions because they will help you, and guide you to make the right decisions.

"It's not just a discovery of space and looking outwards; it's also a journey of self-discovery, especially for Burnham, to understand that if you don't know who you are, and you don't know the emotions you are able to feel, then you don't know yourself. Emotions like love, compassion, and empathy are very powerful, and help us – help the human race – overcome a lot of things. What you choose will define you as a person."

05 T'Kuvma uses the corpse of the Torchbearer to motivate his fellow Klingons.

06 Captain on the bridge.

"That is why we light our beacon this day. To assemble our people. To lock arms against those whose fatal greeting is... 'We come in peace.'"

T'KUVMA

GERSHA PHILLIPS
Costume Designer

"Gretchen [J. Berg, Executive Producer] and Aaron [Harberts, Executive Producer] really always stressed making the show look real… It's a combination of pushing the envelope, but keeping it grounded in reality.

"Predominantly we found pieces that we changed or augmented in some way. So we found things that existed – there are certain designers that are doing some cool futuristic things right now, and we just tried to pull from there…

"For us it was just about keeping it real and making it look futuristic and interesting. I don't wanna use the word 'cool', cos 'cool' is not the right word to say; but it's definitely interesting and wearable – those were the mandates. And more… grounded in reality. I think whenever you go that way, you always produce something that's a little bit better on camera and looks more real." ⋀

BATTLE
AT THE BINARY STARS

SEASON 1, EPISODE 2

First aired: September 24, 2017
Teleplay: Gretchen J. Berg & Aaron Harberts
Story: Bryan Fuller
Director: Adam Kane

CAST

Sonequa Martin-Green: Commander Michael Burnham
Doug Jones: Lieutenant Commander Saru
Michelle Yeoh: Captain Philippa Georgiou
Mary Chieffo: L'Rell
James Frain: Sarek
Kenneth Mitchell: Kol
Chris Obi: T'Kuvma
Terry Serpico: Admiral Brett Anderson
Sam Vartholomeos: Ensign Danby Connor
Arista Arhin: Young Michael Burnham
Emily Coutts: Lieutenant Keyla Detmer
Javid Iqbal (Shazad Latif): Voq
Ali Momen: Lieutenant Kamran Gant
Clare McConnell: Dennas
Thamela Mpumlwana: Young T'Kuvma
Damon Runyan: Ujilli
Tasia Valenza: Computer Voice
Chris Violette: Lieutenant Britch Weeton
Romaine Waite: Lieutenant Troy Januzzi

02

SYNOPSIS

With Michael Burnham consigned to the *U.S.S. Shenzhou* brig for her mutiny, Captain Georgiou attempts to negotiate with the Klingons in order to avert conflict. Her efforts fall on deaf ears: Klingon leader T'Kuvma's intent has always been to instigate a war with the Federation in order to reunite the houses of the fractured Klingon Empire. Accordingly, a peaceful solution was never on the cards.

Before long, the binary star system is the scene of a pitched battle between the massed Klingon fleet and a flotilla of Starfleet vessels. The *U.S.S. Europa*, with Starfleet Admiral Brett Anderson on board, is rammed by a Klingon ship,

> "Why are we fighting? We're Starfleet. We're explorers, not soldiers."
> **DANBY CONNOR**

while the *Shenzhou* is disabled after sustaining heavy damage.

After witnessing the death of her crewmate Danby Connor, Michael Burnham is forced to perform some extravehicular acrobatics in order to escape the wrecked brig and return to the bridge. There, she finds Georgiou plotting vengeance against T'Kuvma. Rather than killing the Klingon leader and turning him into a martyr, Burnham suggests capturing him. Disabling its shields using a bomb hidden within a Klingon corpse, the pair beam across to T'Kuvma's Sarcophagus ship.

The plan fails: Georgiou is killed by T'Kuvma, who in turn is shot dead by Burnham. The Klingons get their martyr, while Burnham is court-martialed, stripped of her rank, and imprisoned for life.

SONEQUA MARTIN-GREEN
Michael Burnham

"When you can see people actually change – whether that be for good or for bad – that's one of the most exciting, exhilarating things about serialized storytelling. Seeing how decisions lead to someone's development. You go on that journey with me, day by day, as I'm being changed, and shifting my decisions by the people that I'm interacting with, by the people I'm serving with and under. These are things that we touch on and, dare I say, in a very visceral way."

AARON HARBERTS
Executive Producer

"There's a scene in the very first episode, where Captain Georgiou says to Burnham, 'I'm going to recommend you for the captain's chair.' That's it, for Michael, who has always thought she knew how she was getting somewhere. It's all about the plans you have in life.

"By the end of the second episode, she makes choices that change her life completely. She's got to find another path… It's a story about finding out who you are, and learning that sometimes the path you thought you'd take isn't the path you are on."

(Previous spread)

01 Captain Georgiou in action aboard the Klingon Sarcophagus ship.

02 Uneasy allies: Georgiou and Burnham get set to beam over to face T'Kuvma.

03

"From my youth on Vulcan, I was raised to believe that service was my purpose. And I carried that conviction to Starfleet. I dreamed of a day when I would command my own vessel and further the noble objectives of this great institution. That dream is over, the only ship I know in ruins."

MICHAEL BURNHAM

03 Georgiou versus T'Kuvma.

04 A younger Burnham with her adoptive father, Sarek (James Frain).

05 Burnham in battle.

06 T'Kuvma surveys his magnificent vessel.

"Commander Burnham, you have endangered your vessel and your shipmates. You have attacked a superior officer. You violated the chain of command. You are relieved of duty."

PHILIPPA GEORGIOU

GLENN HETRICK
Prosthetic and Special FX Make-up

"With the Klingons, as we got closer and closer [to production], I created a cultural axiom document for all the great houses. The concept behind that was, up till now, every house kind of looks the same. Why would that be? If you think about our planet – how many different cultures, and the cultural patina that gives our food or architecture or fashion or jewelry – what would it be like in the Empire? They all grow up on different planets, they don't all grow up on Qo'noS, and they've been spacefaring for how long? We're just this tiny new species, really.

"So we're trying to convey with the Klingons that each house very much has its own individual look, so much so that their skin – if you pay close attention, the delegates that we see in Season 1, in [Episode 2] and then a few later, like Dennas and Ujilli, representatives of House Mo'Kai and House D'Ghor – their skin tones are actually different, just like ours. That's one of those things that started so long ago as just words, and it's played out as a main function of our evolutionary imperative in our design." ⋀

CONTEXT IS FOR KINGS

SEASON 1, EPISODE 3

First aired:
October 1, 2017
Teleplay: Gretchen J. Berg
& Aaron Harberts &
Craig Sweeny
Story: Bryan Fuller &
Gretchen J. Berg &
Aaron Harberts
Director: Akiva Goldsman

CAST

Sonequa Martin-Green:
Michael Burnham
Doug Jones:
Commander Saru
Anthony Rapp:
Lieutenant Paul Stamets
Mary Wiseman:
Cadet Sylvia Tilly
Jason Isaacs:
Captain Gabriel Lorca
Rekha Sharma:
Commander Ellen Landry
Emily Coutts:
Lieutenant Keyla Detmer
Julianne Grossman:
Discovery Computer
Grace Lynn Kung: Psycho
Devon MacDonald:
Engineering Officer
Sara Mitich: Lieutenant
Commander Airiam
Oyin Oladejo: Lieutenant
Joann Owosekun
Conrad Pla: Stone
Ronnie Rowe Jr.:
Shuttle Pilot
Christopher Russell:
Lieutenant Milton Richter
Saad Siddiqui: Straal
Elias Toufexis: Cold
Tasia Valenza:
Shenzhou Computer

01

SYNOPSIS

Rescued from a stricken shuttle along with a trio of fellow prisoners, Michael Burnham finds herself aboard a gleaming new ship: the *U.S.S. Discovery*. Having achieved a level of infamy across the Federation for starting the war with the Klingons – a war that has already cost upwards of 8,000 souls – Burnham is met by cold stares and suspicion.

After being introduced to the ship's captain, Gabriel Lorca – who seems to already know rather a lot about her – Burnham is quartered with Cadet Sylvia Tilly. She is also reunited with her former friend – and the *Shenzhou*'s former science officer – Saru. Now *Discovery*'s first officer, the Kelpien regards her as a danger.

> "I'm not here by accident. I think you brought me here. I think you've been testing me."
>
> **MICHAEL BURNHAM TO GABRIEL LORCA**

Tasked with assisting *Discovery*'s chief engineer, Lieutenant Paul Stamets, with a project, Burnham breaks into his lab and finds the room is filled with strange alien fungi. Meanwhile, *Discovery*'s sister ship, the *U.S.S. Glenn*, has suffered an "incident" during its last "black alert." Burnham joins Stamets, Tilly, security chief Landry, and a security officer on an away mission to the other ship, where they find the *Glenn*'s crew dead and a giant carnivorous monster on the loose. The security officer is killed, but the rest of the away team escape with their lives.

Back on *Discovery*, Lorca reveals to Burnham that his ship is an experimental vessel developing a "spore drive" that will revolutionize space travel – and could win the war with the Klingons. After giving her a taste of its potential, Lorca offers Burnham a place in his crew.

(Previous spread)

01 Captain Gabriel Lorca assumes a commanding position.

02 Broken, bowed: Michael Burnham, commander no more.

AARON HARBERTS
Executive Producer

"I really loved Episode 3, because it was willing to show us a lead of *Star Trek* that had been truly broken down to nothing, and it set up a journey of humanity that ultimately paid off by the 15th episode."

SONEQUA MARTIN-GREEN
Michael Burnham

"This is a story of a lot of things. It's a story of failure and victory. It's a story of fear. It's a story of love and of guilt. It's a story of redemption, of restoration, and of reconciliation and of degradation. I think it's a lot of those things, but all the while maintaining the hope and optimism that is *Star Trek*.

"I truly think it's high-quality storytelling. We are able to explore all these themes simultaneously. The only reason we're able to do that is the long-form storytelling that is offered by the digital-streaming platform. That's one of the beautiful things about this iteration of *Star Trek*, is that we're able to do that, that we're able to go to those darkest places while still keeping the light on, if you will. We're able to build on what's introduced into the story. Everything has ramifications. These are high-stakes consequences."

"I did choose you, but not for the reasons you think... You chose to do the right thing over what was sanctioned, even at great cost to yourself. And that is the kind of thinking that wins wars. The kind of thinking I need next to me. Universal law is for lackeys. Context... is for kings."

GABRIEL LORCA TO MICHAEL BURNHAM

AKIVA GOLDSMAN
Executive Producer

"The sets are larger than people imagine. More of the show is actually shot practically. A lot of what we're seeing these days, a lot of big science fiction movies and television shows, have a tremendous amount of digital set extension. But our sets are for real. I've rarely seen sets this big, this articulated, this complex, and this staggering.

"What happens then is that the action can be very organic, as if they're really occupying the ship. I think it's unprecedented. I've never seen *Star Trek* sets as practically executed." ∧

03 Michael Burnham encounters Lieutenant Paul Stamets.

04 Lieutenant Stamets: usually the smartest guy in the room.

05 Saru, now *Discovery*'s Number One.

06 The chosen one: Burnham is perplexed by Lorca's interest in her.

07 Burnham in her new *Discovery* quarters.

THE BUTCHER'S KNIFE CARES NOT FOR THE LAMB'S CRY

SEASON 1, EPISODE 4

First aired:
October 8, 2017
Writers: Jesse Alexander
& Aron Eli Coleite
Director:
Olatunde Osunsanmi

CAST

Sonequa Martin-Green:
Michael Burnham
Doug Jones:
Commander Saru
Anthony Rapp:
Lieutenant Paul Stamets
Mary Wiseman:
Cadet Sylvia Tilly
Jason Isaacs:
Captain Gabriel Lorca
Michelle Yeoh: Captain
Philippa Georgiou
Jayne Brook: Admiral
Katrina Cornwell
Mary Chieffo: L'Rell
**Javid Iqbal (Shazad
Latif):** Voq
Wilson Cruz:
Doctor Hugh Culber
Kenneth Mitchell: Kol
Rekha Sharma:
Commander Ellen Landry
Dennis Andres:
Engineer Rance
Emily Coutts:
Lieutenant Keyla Detmer
Sara Mitich: Lieutenant
Commander Airiam
Oyin Oladejo: Lieutenant
Joann Owosekun
Christopher Russell:
Lieutenant Milton Richter

SYNOPSIS

With T'Kuvma consigned to the history books, Voq has taken on responsibility for his leader's great task. Unfortunately, the Sarcophagus ship is drifting in space, marooned, and with a starving crew – so hungry, in fact, that they've already made a meal of Captain Georgiou's corpse.

Beaming aboard the Sarcophagus ship, General Kol quickly ousts Voq and takes control. L'Rell, Voq's trusted acolyte – or so he believed – switches sides in an instant, leaving Voq literally out in the cold. At least, so it appears…

Aboard *Discovery*, Burnham has been tasked with weaponizing the dangerous tardigrade

> "I do not want the mantle of leadership. Standing behind you, I am free to move. Able to be your enforcer, defender, campaigner."
>
> **L'RELL TO VOQ**

creature recovered from the *U.S.S. Glenn* – an assignment that takes an alarming turn when Commander Landry rashly intercedes and is promptly killed by the creature. Noticing the tardigrade's distress during every black alert, Burnham theorizes that the beast has some connection with the spore drive, and presents her ideas to Lieutenant Stamets.

It transpires that "Ripper" – as the unfortunate Landry named it – has a symbiotic relationship with the mycelial network, using it to navigate its way through the universe – which is precisely what *Discovery*'s spore drive needs. With the tardigrade hooked up to the drive, *Discovery* jumps to the embattled Corvan II to save the colonists there from a Klingon attack.

TAMARA DEVERELL
Production Designer

[On the dichotomy between the *U.S.S. Discovery* and ships in previous iterations of *Trek*:] "Part of it is the technology we have now to build things, like CNC cutting and laser printing and all of that – LED lights that we can use throughout the set so the set's lighting itself. We can't turn our backs to that and do justice to the fans and the audience. So you have to make that leap of faith with us, that we're gonna create a spectacular-looking bunch of sets, but we're gonna try and bring in the essence of what *Star Trek* has offered up before.

"Although the *Discovery* bridge set was done before my time, in the sets subsequent to that, there's a lot of the same sort of doorways and archways, and the overall architectural details. A ship is round – the *Discovery* itself is a round disk – so the sets are round – we can't get away from that. So you end up embracing that and having a lot of the same architectural elements, like curved beams and so on.

"But now, instead of old *Star Trek* where there's a curved beam, or in the *Next Gen* or whatever, ours have lights in them, and LED lights. Then we can do black alerts, so everything's just pushed to the next level. If we started doing sets that weren't so much more far advanced than previous *Star Trek*s, then the audience would actually be disappointed. So you're going to have to forgive us a little bit."

> "You're new here; so let me share a piece of wisdom. Lorca isn't interested in what you are. He's interested in what you can do. For him."
>
> **ELLEN LANDRY TO MICHAEL BURNHAM**

06

MARY CHIEFFO
L'Rell

"One surprise early on, that then manifested in L'Rell, was the softness. I remember filming Episode 4 and feeling that we were getting this intimacy that I didn't necessarily expect. We were still filming the season when those early episodes started airing, and I remember when Episode 4 came out, I had no idea that she was *that* vulnerable in certain moments. I think I had the last three or four episodes left to film, so it empowered me to really embrace that, as I took those last few scenes and moments.

"The [make-up] helped a lot in manifesting exactly how she carried herself. I did a lot of mask and movement work in college, and that was definitely something I leaned on in this very outside-in experience. But at the same time, what was so beautiful when it came to the scenes as they were writing them, particularly Episode 4 onward, was that there was room to find a softness and vulnerability, despite the fact that she's this intimidating-looking Klingon." ⋏

03 The *U.S.S. Discovery* bridge in all its glory.

04 Burnham and Landry discuss the tardigrade.

05 Saru in Engineering.

06 Saru brings Burnham to the bridge.

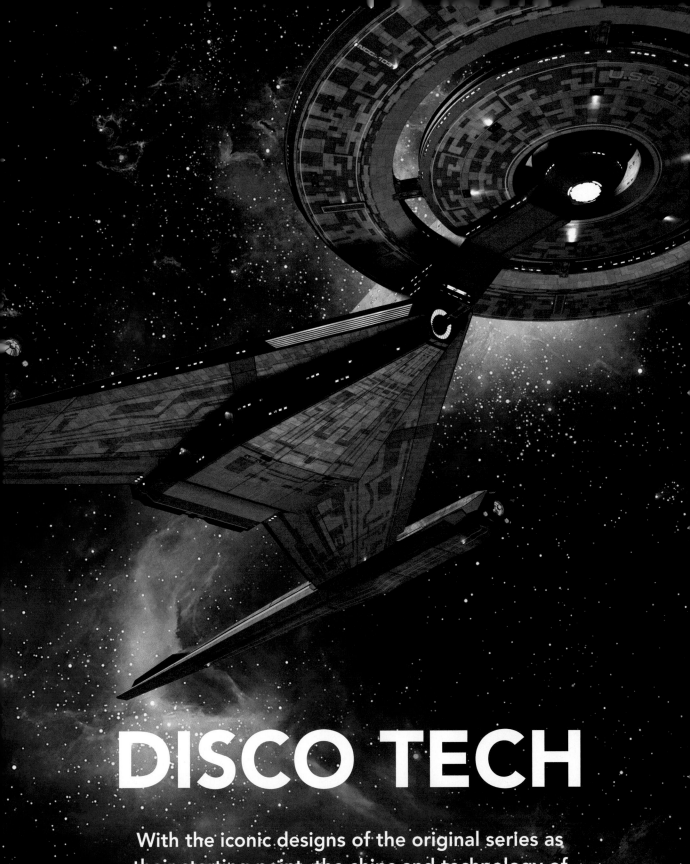

DISCO TECH

With the iconic designs of the original series as
their starting point, the ships and technology of
Star Trek: Discovery strike a balance between the
1960s futurism of the Kirk era and a plausible vision
of 23rd Century vessels, weapons, and devices.

U.S.S. DISCOVERY

NCC-1031

Class: *Crossfield*
Captain: Gabriel Lorca
First Officer: Saru
Motto: "All things can be understood once they are discovered; the point is to discover them."
First appearance: Episode 3, "Context Is for Kings"

Ventral view ▲

Left view ◢

Dorsal view ▼

Ventral view ▼

Front view ▲

"If the *Discovery* can be anywhere and gone in an instant, that's how you beat the Klingons. That's how you win the war. And we must win the war. But that's just the beginning. Imagine the possibilities."

CAPTAIN GABRIEL LORCA

U.S.S. SHENZHOU

N C C - 1 2 2 7

Class: *Walker*
Captain: Philippa Georgiou
First Officer: Michael Burnham
Motto: "All existing things are really one."
First appearance: Episode 1, "The Vulcan Hello"

Dorsal view △

Left view △

Aft view △

Dorsal view ▽

Ventral view ▽

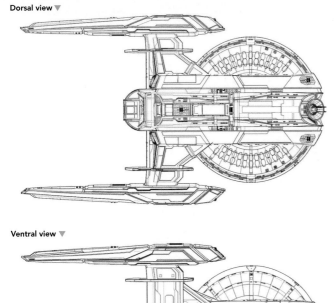

> "*Shenzhou* is old, but she gets us where we need to go."
> **CAPTAIN PHILIPPA GEORGIOU**

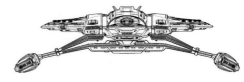

Aft view △

Right view △

HASER

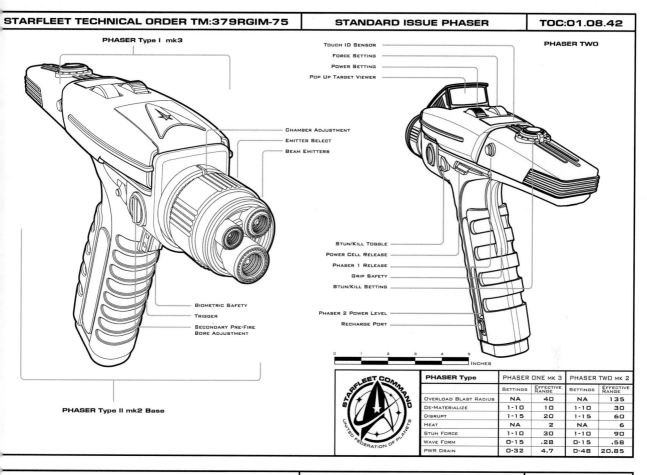

PHASER Type I mk3

TOUCH ID SENSOR
FORCE SETTING
POWER SETTING
POP UP TARGET VIEWER

PHASER TWO

CHAMBER ADJUSTMENT
EMITTER SELECT
BEAM EMITTERS

BIOMETRIC SAFETY
TRIGGER
SECONDARY PRE-FIRE
BORE ADJUSTMENT

PHASER Type II mk2 Base

STUN/KILL TOGGLE
POWER CELL RELEASE
PHASER 1 RELEASE
GRIP SAFETY
STUN/KILL SETTING

PHASER 2 POWER LEVEL
RECHARGE PORT

0 1 2 3 4 5 INCHES

STARFLEET COMMAND · UNITED FEDERATION OF PLANETS

PHASER Type	PHASER ONE MK 3		PHASER TWO MK 2	
	SETTINGS	EFFECTIVE RANGE	SETTINGS	EFFECTIVE RANGE
OVERLOAD BLAST RADIUS	NA	40	NA	135
DE-MATERIALIZE	1-10	10	1-10	30
DISRUPT	1-15	20	1-15	60
HEAT	NA	2	NA	6
STUN FORCE	1-10	30	1-10	90
WAVE FORM	0-15	.28	0-15	.58
PWR DRAIN	0-32	4.7	0-48	20.85

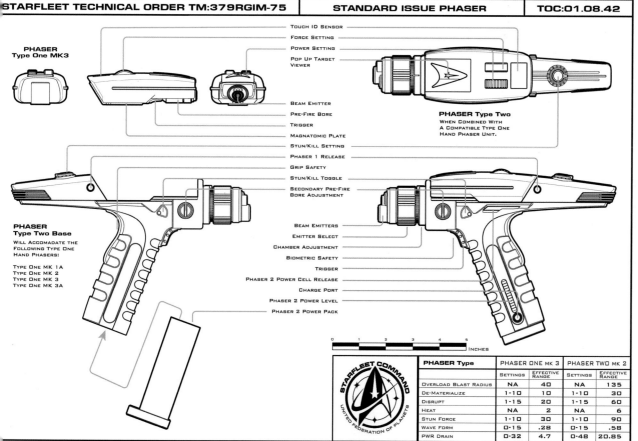

PHASER
Type One MK3

TOUCH ID SENSOR
FORCE SETTING
POWER SETTING
POP UP TARGET VIEWER

BEAM EMITTER
PRE-FIRE BORE
TRIGGER
MAGNATOMIC PLATE
STUN/KILL SETTING
PHASER 1 RELEASE
GRIP SAFETY
STUN/KILL TOGGLE
SECONDARY PRE-FIRE
BORE ADJUSTMENT

BEAM EMITTERS
EMITTER SELECT
CHAMBER ADJUSTMENT
BIOMETRIC SAFETY
TRIGGER
PHASER 2 POWER CELL RELEASE
CHARGE PORT
PHASER 2 POWER LEVEL
PHASER 2 POWER PACK

PHASER Type Two
WHEN COMBINED WITH
A COMPATIBLE TYPE ONE
HAND PHASER UNIT.

**PHASER
Type Two Base**
WILL ACCOMADATE THE
FOLLOWING TYPE ONE
HAND PHASERS:

TYPE ONE MK 1A
TYPE ONE MK 2
TYPE ONE MK 3
TYPE ONE MK 3A

0 1 2 3 4 5 INCHES

STARFLEET COMMAND · UNITED FEDERATION OF PLANETS

PHASER Type	PHASER ONE MK 3		PHASER TWO MK 2	
	SETTINGS	EFFECTIVE RANGE	SETTINGS	EFFECTIVE RANGE
OVERLOAD BLAST RADIUS	NA	40	NA	135
DE-MATERIALIZE	1-10	10	1-10	30
DISRUPT	1-15	20	1-15	60
HEAT	NA	2	NA	6
STUN FORCE	1-10	30	1-10	90
WAVE FORM	0-15	.28	0-15	.58
PWR DRAIN	0-32	4.7	0-48	20.85

COMMUNICATOR

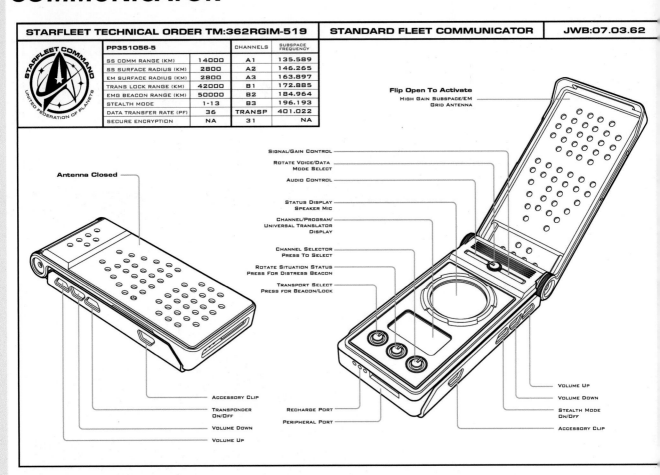

PP351056-5		CHANNELS	SUBSPACE FREQUENCY
SS COMM RANGE (KM)	14000	A1	135.589
SS SURFACE RADIUS (KM)	2800	A2	146.265
EM SURFACE RADIUS (KM)	2800	A3	163.897
TRANS LOCK RANGE (KM)	42000	B1	172.885
EMG BEACON RANGE (KM)	50000	B2	184.964
STEALTH MODE	1-13	B3	196.193
DATA TRANSFER RATE (PF)	36	TRANSP	401.022
SECURE ENCRYPTION	NA	31	NA

Flip Open To Activate
HIGH GAIN SUBSPACE/EM GRID ANTENNA

Antenna Closed

SIGNAL/GAIN CONTROL
ROTATE VOICE/DATA MODE SELECT
AUDIO CONTROL

STATUS DISPLAY SPEAKER MIC
CHANNEL/PROGRAM/ UNIVERSAL TRANSLATOR DISPLAY

CHANNEL SELECTOR PRESS TO SELECT
ROTATE SITUATION STATUS PRESS FOR DISTRESS BEACON
TRANSPORT SELECT PRESS FOR BEACON/LOCK

ACCESSORY CLIP
TRANSPONDER ON/OFF
VOLUME DOWN
VOLUME UP

RECHARGE PORT
PERIPHERAL PORT

VOLUME UP
VOLUME DOWN
STEALTH MODE ON/OFF
ACCESSORY CLIP

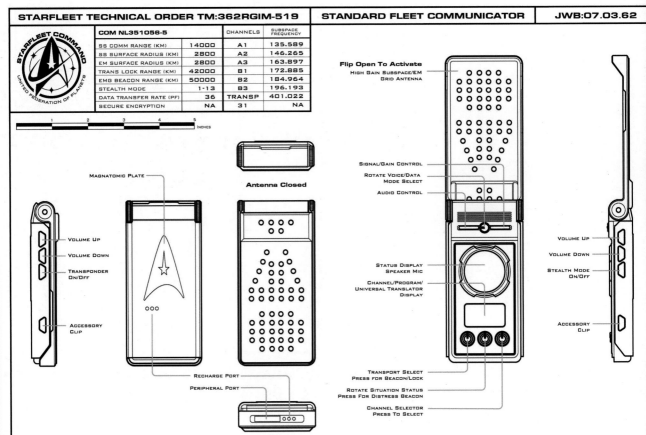

COM NL351056-5		CHANNELS	SUBSPACE FREQUENCY
SS COMM RANGE (KM)	14000	A1	135.589
SS SURFACE RADIUS (KM)	2800	A2	146.265
EM SURFACE RADIUS (KM)	2800	A3	163.897
TRANS LOCK RANGE (KM)	42000	B1	172.885
EMG BEACON RANGE (KM)	50000	B2	184.964
STEALTH MODE	1-13	B3	196.193
DATA TRANSFER RATE (PF)	36	TRANSP	401.022
SECURE ENCRYPTION	NA	31	NA

1 2 3 4 5
INCHES

MAGNATOMIC PLATE

Antenna Closed

Flip Open To Activate
HIGH GAIN SUBSPACE/EM GRID ANTENNA

SIGNAL/GAIN CONTROL
ROTATE VOICE/DATA MODE SELECT
AUDIO CONTROL

VOLUME UP
VOLUME DOWN
TRANSPONDER ON/OFF

ACCESSORY CLIP

STATUS DISPLAY SPEAKER MIC
CHANNEL/PROGRAM/ UNIVERSAL TRANSLATOR DISPLAY

VOLUME UP
VOLUME DOWN
STEALTH MODE ON/OFF

ACCESSORY CLIP

RECHARGE PORT
PERIPHERAL PORT

TRANSPORT SELECT PRESS FOR BEACON/LOCK
ROTATE SITUATION STATUS PRESS FOR DISTRESS BEACON
CHANNEL SELECTOR PRESS TO SELECT

TRICORDER

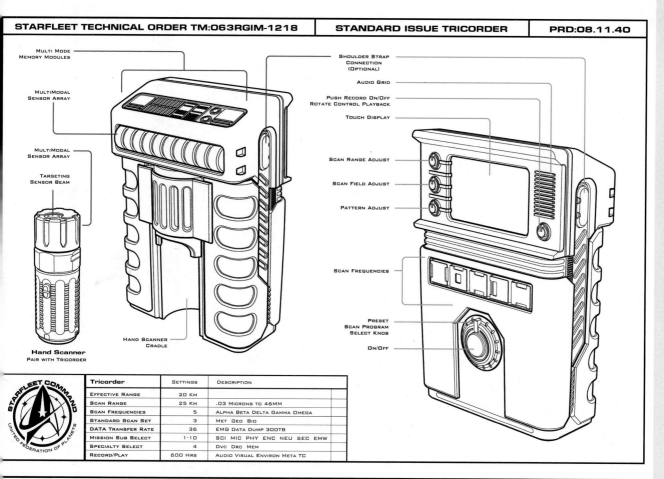

Multi Mode Memory Modules

MultiModal Sensor Array

MultiModal Sensor Array

Targeting Sensor Beam

Shoulder Strap Connection (Optional)

Audio Grid

Push Record On/Off Rotate Control Playback

Touch Display

Scan Range Adjust

Scan Field Adjust

Pattern Adjust

Scan Frequencies

Preset Scan Program Select Knob

On/Off

Hand Scanner Cradle

Hand Scanner
PAIR WITH TRICORDER

Tricorder	Settings	Description
Effective Range	20 Km	
Scan Range	25 Km	.03 Microns to 46MM
Scan Frequencies	5	Alpha Beta Delta Gamma Omega
Standard Scan Set	3	Met Geo Bio
Data Transfer Rate	36	EMG Data Dump 300TB
Mission Sub Select	1-10	Sci Mic Phy Enc Neu Sec EMW
Specialty Select	4	Dvc Drc Mem
Record/Play	600 Hrs	Audio Visual Environ Meta TC

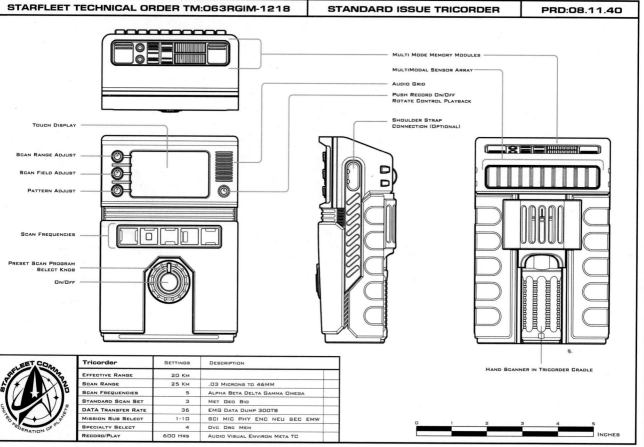

Multi Mode Memory Modules

MultiModal Sensor Array

Audio Grid

Push Record On/Off Rotate Control Playback

Shoulder Strap Connection (Optional)

Touch Display

Scan Range Adjust

Scan Field Adjust

Pattern Adjust

Scan Frequencies

Preset Scan Program Select Knob

On/Off

Hand Scanner in Tricorder Cradle

Tricorder	Settings	Description
Effective Range	20 Km	
Scan Range	25 Km	.03 Microns to 46MM
Scan Frequencies	5	Alpha Beta Delta Gamma Omega
Standard Scan Set	3	Met Geo Bio
Data Transfer Rate	36	EMG Data Dump 300TB
Mission Sub Select	1-10	Sci Mic Phy Enc Neu Sec EMW
Specialty Select	4	Dvc Drc Mem
Record/Play	600 Hrs	Audio Visual Environ Meta TC

0 1 2 3 4 5 INCHES

CHOOSE YOUR PAIN

SEASON 1, EPISODE 5

First aired:
October 15, 2017
Teleplay: Kemp Powers
Story: Gretchen J. Berg
& Aaron Harberts &
Kemp Powers
Director: Lee Rose

CAST

Sonequa Martin-Green:
Michael Burnham
Doug Jones:
Commander Saru
Shazad Latif:
Lieutenant Ash Tyler
Anthony Rapp:
Lieutenant Paul Stamets
Mary Wiseman:
Cadet Sylvia Tilly
Jason Isaacs:
Captain Gabriel Lorca
Jayne Brook: Admiral
Katrina Cornwell
Mary Chieffo: L'Rell
Wilson Cruz:
Doctor Hugh Culber
Rainn Wilson:
Harry Mudd
Conrad Coates:
Admiral Terral
Emily Coutts:
Lieutenant Keyla Detmer
Patrick Kwok-Choon:
Lieutenant Rhys
Sara Mitich: Lieutenant
Commander Airiam
Oyin Oladejo: Lieutenant
Joann Owosekun
Christopher Russell:
Lieutenant Milton Richter

01

SYNOPSIS

A s Michael Burnham suffers from bad dreams, the tardigrade's health deteriorates – the result, Burnham surmises, of plugging the creature into the *Discovery* spore drive. Meanwhile, Lorca is summoned before a group of admirals and ordered to scale back the use of the spore drive, lest the Klingons identify *Discovery* as Starfleet's secret weapon.

En route back to his ship, Lorca is attacked by Klingons and taken prisoner. Dumped in a dank cell, the captain is surprised to meet not only a loquacious individual named Harcourt Fenton Mudd, but also Ash Tyler, a wounded Starfleet officer held prisoner by the Klingons for seven months. Leaving the duplicitous

> "We choose our own pain. Mine helps me remember."
> **GABRIEL LORCA**

Mudd to his fate, Lorca and Tyler escape, battling their way past numerous warriors to steal a Klingon raider.

Having stepped up to take command of *Discovery*, Saru instigates a dangerous search for his captain, but his efforts are thwarted when the spore drive fails following a jump into Klingon space. The tardigrade has fallen into a state of extreme cryptobiosis, and Burnham, Tilly, and Stamets race to find a solution. As *Discovery* intercepts a squadron of Klingon raiders, Stamets injects himself with the tardigrade's DNA and hooks himself up to the spore drive, taking the ship to black alert as Lorca and Tyler are beamed to safety.

However, Stamets' radical solution seems to have had some very unexpected side effects…

(Previous
spread)

01 A captured
Captain Lorca
is interrogated
by L'Rell.

02 Rainn
Wilson as
Harcourt
Fenton Mudd.

GERSHA PHILLIPS
Costume Designer

"The only person who wanted
something different [for their
uniform], and maybe even
transformed it into what he
needed it to be, was Jason
Isaacs. He definitely walks his
own path. It was interesting,
because I was trying to figure
out just lately if Jason is like
that, or if it's part of his
character, Lorca. I feel like
it's more of his character and
that's what we were all living
with at the time. So it was
interesting, because when an
actor wears it like that, you're always kind
of confused.

"He was the one who really wanted to
wear his jacket open; he wanted to wear a gun,
a phaser. So there were some really interesting
choices that he wanted to make that were
different than anybody else's. He was the one
person who was like, 'Okay, I'm gonna wear this
open.' And then we had to redesign it cos it's

> "I used to have a
> life, Captain, a good
> one. A respectable
> business. That
> all got blown up,
> because of your
> goddamn war."
>
> **HARRY MUDD
> TO GABRIEL LORCA**

asymmetrical, so it doesn't really
look great open."

JASON ISAACS
Captain Gabriel Lorca

"If you don't have secrets to play,
you have nothing to play on
camera… Nobody interesting on-
camera ever says what they mean,
and nobody ever fully understands
themselves. When I've played
real life characters in the past,
meeting them and talking to them
is completely useless. Meeting
their family, their friends, their
enemies, and the people they work
with is the way to build up a three-
dimensional picture of someone.

"Lorca maybe doesn't know himself, or
thinks he knows himself, and is trying to
do the job of a leader, which is sometimes
manipulating, sometimes bullying, sometimes
encouraging. And it's in a time of war. If you
look at the news around us, leaders are having
a tough time leading their people, and I have a
tough time too."

03

03 Burnham offers words of encouragement to Saru.

04 Lorca meets Mudd.

05 Burnham, lost in thought.

06 Ash Tyler looks on while Mudd expounds.

RAINN WILSON
Harry Mudd

"I inherited a character that had been previously played by a brilliant actor. I stole a lot of things that I loved from his performance, and then added a lot more of my own. It's a testament to [original series Mudd] Roger C. Carmel, to what an interesting actor he was. You can't take your eyes off him when he's in an episode. He's so full of light. The new writers have added that he's mischievous and deadly at the same time, and that's a fun balance to watch." ⌃

01

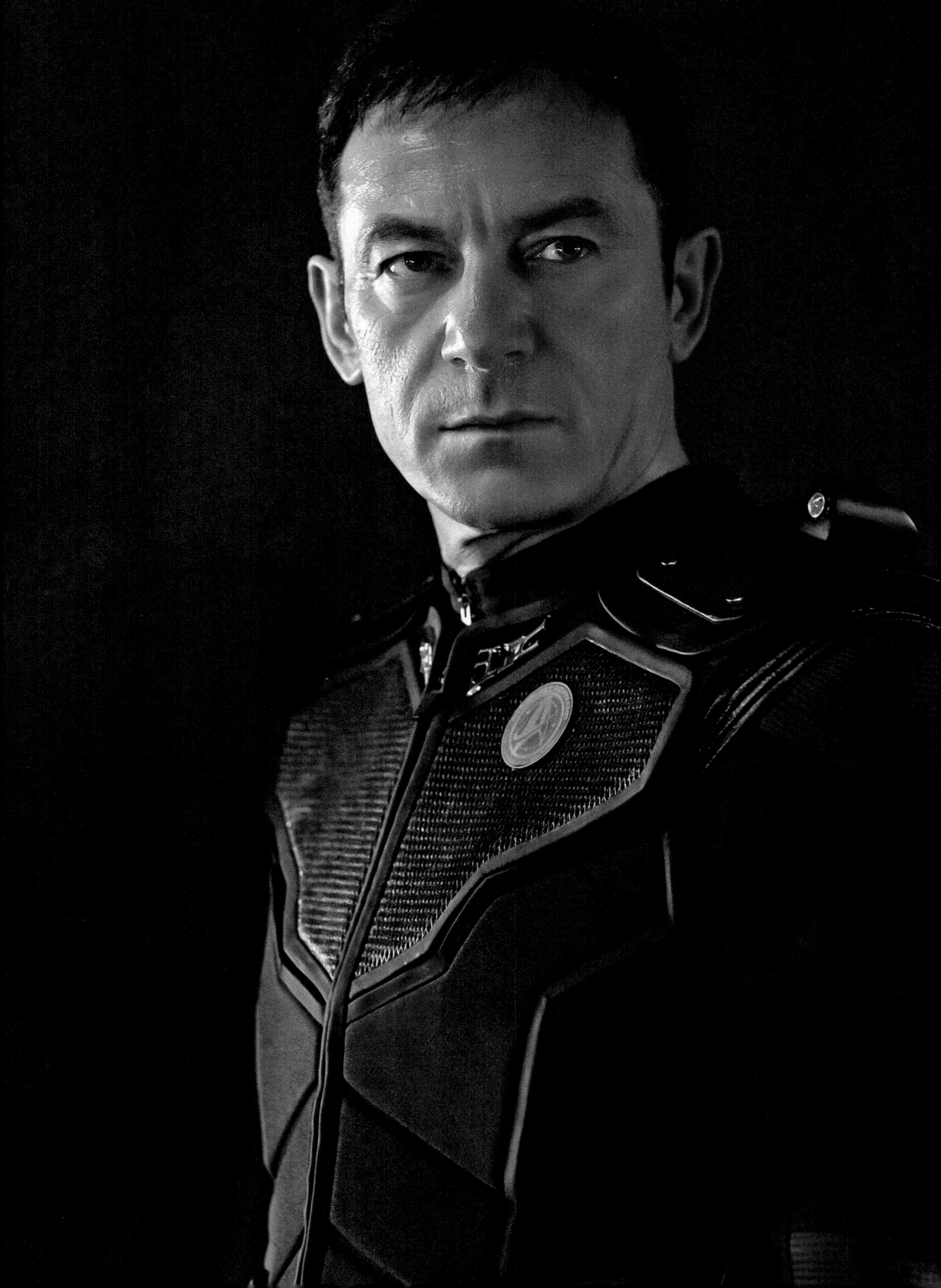

LETHE

SEASON 1, EPISODE 6

First aired:
October 22, 2017
Writers: Joe Menosky
& Ted Sullivan
Director: Douglas
Aarniokoski

CAST

Sonequa Martin-Green:
Michael Burnham
Doug Jones:
Commander Saru
Shazad Latif:
Lieutenant Ash Tyler
Anthony Rapp:
Lieutenant Paul Stamets
Mary Wiseman:
Cadet Sylvia Tilly
Jason Isaacs:
Captain Gabriel Lorca
Jayne Brook: Admiral
Katrina Cornwell
Wilson Cruz:
Doctor Hugh Culber
James Frain: Sarek
Mia Kirshner:
Amanda Grayson
Kenneth Mitchell: Kol
Conrad Coates:
Admiral Terral
Emily Coutts:
Lieutenant Keyla Detmer
Luke Humphrey:
V'Latak
Clare McConnell:
Dennas
Sara Mitich: Lieutenant
Commander Airiam
Oyin Oladejo:
Lieutenant Joann
Owosekun
Damon Runyan: Ujilli
Jonathan Whittaker:
Vulcan Director

SYNOPSIS

Sarek, Michael Burnham's adoptive father, is in trouble. Injured and lost in deep space following an assassination attempt, his unconscious mind reaches out to his daughter for help. Captain Lorca gives Burnham permission to take a shuttle and find her father, who was on a diplomatic mission to broker peace between the Klingons and the Federation.

Back on *Discovery*, Admiral Cornwell pays a visit, concerned about her old friend, Lorca, who has been acting out of character, to the point where she's considering removing him from command. As "officers with benefits," they soon

> "Rules are for admirals and back offices. I'm out there trying to win a war."
>
> **GABRIEL LORCA**

forget their differences, but the mood is broken when Cornwell discovers Lorca sleeps with a phaser under his pillow.

Still searching for Sarek, Burnham is led ever closer to her father by a series of long-distance mind melds. But she uncovers a shattering secret, one that the Vulcan has withheld from Burnham for many years.

With the peace conference due to begin, and Sarek in no state to lead the talks, Lorca suggests Cornwell go in his place, as she's the highest-ranking officer. When the Klingons' peace overtures turn out to be a trap, Lorca regrets that without orders he cannot authorize a rescue of the kidnapped Cornwell – thus handily forestalling her actions against him.

(Previous spread)

01 Captain Gabriel Lorca, ready for combat.

02 Tyler and Lorca get ready to breach a door during a holographic battle simulation.

GRETCHEN J. BERG
Executive Producer

"We have so many people [on staff] who are *Trek* fans and worship at the church of it, practically. So we're not reckless – we're never being reckless – but I think a lot of times what we're trying to do is challenge the known canon and get a story out of it. But our intention is never to blow things up in a reckless way. We take the show, and the history of the show, and what it is, and what it means to people, very, very seriously."

AARON HARBERTS
Executive Producer

"We have a writing staff that really keeps us honest, but then what we have to say is, 'Okay, but let's challenge ourselves.' If you throw up all of these walls you're not gonna get anywhere, so let's be creative – how can we get around it? How can we pay it off later, and show the audience that we knew what we were doing?

"Normally when we do that it is all about saying, a few episodes down the line, 'See, we knew.' And because the

episodes really were created as a unit, it wasn't like, 'Oh and then we messed that up so we need to fix it now.' We kind of knew how we were gonna do that along the way, and that's one of the things we're excited about for Season 2, because there are still many questions the audience is gonna have about how *Discovery* exists in the timeline – these stories about Michael Burnham and her adopted Vulcan family.

"There's lots of stuff that we want to do next season in terms of making sure that *Discovery* has a very important and secure place in our timeline and in canon, without breaking what everybody loves about it."

> "Don't take my ship away from me. She's all I got. Please, I'm begging you."
>
> **GABRIEL LORCA TO KATRINA CORNWELL**

JAMES FRAIN
Sarek

"It's really demanding to have your emotional life so completely in check. [*Laughs*] Sometimes I feel like I'm not doing much, but the producers are like, 'No. You're fine. You're not moving an inch.' I'm like, 'Okay. Good. That should do it.'

"It's really interesting, the Vulcan ideal where they came to the conclusion that emotion, all emotion, is a problem. That is so alien to us. Ultimately, is it really achievable? And who is this alien guy that marries a human being? I mean, how did that happen? Answering that is what I feel like I'm doing every day." ▲

03 Lorca, Burnham, and the *Discovery* bridge crew ponder how to find Sarek.

04 Lorca and Tyler, side by side in simulated combat.

05 Lorca and Admiral Cornwell: officers with benefits.

06 Ash Tyler at the ready.

MAGIC TO MAKE THE SANEST MAN GO MAD

01

SEASON 1, EPISODE 7

First aired:
October 29, 2017
Writers: Aron Eli Coleite
& Jesse Alexander
Director: David M. Barrett

CAST

Sonequa Martin-Green:
Michael Burnham
Doug Jones:
Commander Saru
Shazad Latif:
Lieutenant Ash Tyler
Anthony Rapp:
Lieutenant Paul Stamets
Mary Wiseman:
Cadet Sylvia Tilly
Jason Isaacs:
Captain Gabriel Lorca
Wilson Cruz:
Doctor Hugh Culber
Katherine Barrell:
Stella Grimes
Pete MacNeill:
Barron Grimes
Rainn Wilson:
Harry Mudd
Emily Coutts:
Lieutenant Keyla Detmer
Patrick Kwok-Choon:
Lieutenant Rhys
Sara Mitich: Lieutenant
Commander Airiam
Oyin Oladejo: Lieutenant
Joann Owosekun

SYNOPSIS

S lowly settling into life aboard *Discovery*, Michael Burnham must face her greatest fear: a party! Even worse, it's an experience she will be forced to endure again, and again, and again...

Of the *Discovery* crew, Lieutenant Paul Stamets is the only one who can see what's happening – an unanticipated side effect of connecting himself to the ship's spore drive. Afforded a unique perspective on reality, the scientist recognizes a time loop when he sees one – and he and the rest of *Discovery*'s crew are stuck in one now. Unfortunately, he can't deal with the situation on his own, and he hasn't slept in days.

"Do you know how many times I've had the pleasure of taking your life, Lorca? Fifty-three. But who's counting?"

HARRY MUDD

Through repeated attempts, Stamets manages to make Burnham aware of the time loop (even giving her a dance lesson into the bargain). It turns out that Harry Mudd is responsible for controlling the loop, which is generated by an alien gauntlet he's using to incrementally piece together information about *Discovery*. Harry, it seems, has done a deal with the Klingons, who have set him free on the condition that he delivers *Discovery*'s secrets to them.

However, Harry grows increasingly frustrated by the interference of Burnham, Stamets, and Ash Tyler, who hatch a scheme to break the loop and put time back on their side. The thwarted Mudd is left to a suitable punishment: a reunion with his beloved Stella.

(Previous spread)

01 Tyler and Burnham stalk a *Discovery* out of their control.

02 Harry Mudd takes command.

AARON HARBERTS
Executive Producer

"Gretchen J. Berg and I have made no secret of the fact that we are new to the *Trek* family, and we thought that the fans might expect a very rigid and serious tone from the show. However, when you watch a lot of the episodes of *TNG*, and you watch *Voyager*, and of course the original series, there is humor. There's certainly room for that, but out of the gate we just thought, 'Oh people are gonna want serious *Star Trek*, they wanna know that we're taking care of that.'

"And then when Episode 7 aired – the time-loop episode – you definitely got to see that people were excited about it and were welcoming of that [more comedic] tone. And we love to write that. Most of our career has been spent on shows that have a blended tone, and comedy that comes out of character, so not just jokes, but like, why are Burnham and Saru just funny together right out of the gate? Y'know, Tilly and Burnham's characters just lend themselves to the sort of 'odd couple' vibe.

"We wanna do more of it; I think that the fact that people were so embracing of it and accepting of it encouraged us to be able to say, 'It doesn't have to be all serious all the time.'"

GRETCHEN J. BERG
Executive Producer

"[Comedy is] always about when it's appropriate or not. Our cast does comedy so well, and they're very grounded in it; we love writing it, our entire staff loves writing it."

> "I am among the others, but also apart. I wish sorely to step out of my comfort zone, yet don't know how. But tonight, I will face one of my greatest challenges so far. Tonight, we are having... a party."
>
> **MICHAEL BURNHAM**

03 Michael Burnham at the *Disco* disco.

04 Mudd's woman: Stella Grimes (Katherine Barrell) catches up with her errant husband-to-be.

05 The *Discovery* crew contemplate the trouble with Harry.

06 At the mercy of Mudd.

MARIO MOREIRA
Props Master

"My favorite Easter egg that we put into the show was the Andorian helmet that Mudd wears in this episode. It was inspired by, and it was completely in honor of, the original series episode 'Journey to Babel,' where the Andorian was actually an Orion in disguise, so the idea of someone disguising themselves as an Andorian was a little bit of an Easter egg for the fans." ⅄

SI VIS PACEM, PARA BELLUM

SEASON 1, EPISODE 8

First aired: November 5, 2017
Writer: Kirsten Beyer
Director: John S. Scott

CAST

Sonequa Martin-Green: Michael Burnham
Doug Jones: Commander Saru
Shazad Latif: Lieutenant Ash Tyler
Anthony Rapp: Lieutenant Paul Stamets
Mary Wiseman: Cadet Sylvia Tilly
Jason Isaacs: Captain Gabriel Lorca
Jayne Brook: Admiral Katrina Cornwell
Mary Chieffo: L'Rell
Wilson Cruz: Doctor Hugh Culber
Kenneth Mitchell: Kol
Michael Boisvert: Captain T'Shen Kovil
Conrad Coates: Admiral Terral
Emily Coutts: Lieutenant Keyla Detmer
Patrick Kwok-Choon: Lieutenant Rhys
Sara Mitich: Lieutenant Commander Airiam
Oyin Oladejo: Lieutenant Joann Owosekun
Ronnie Rowe Jr.: Lieutenant R. A. Bryce

02

SYNOPSIS

As part of a mission vital to the war effort, Michael Burnham, Ash Tyler, and Saru beam down to the planet Pahvo, a world whose unique ecology combines to generate a global music that is transmitted into space via towering crystalline structures. Starfleet hopes to retune the signal emitted by Pahvo's naturally-occurring transmitters and use it as a form of SONAR, negating the Klingons' cloaking technology and making their ships visible to sensors.

Shortly after arriving, the away team encounters a sentient lifeform that manifests as a cloud of glowing blue particles. Able to communicate with this being, Saru is overcome by a sense of peace and calm he feels through his

> "Our futures look different. You go back to your lake house, and I go back to prison. My sentence was life. This is just temporary."
>
> **MICHAEL BURNHAM TO ASH TYLER**

interactions with it, and begins placing obstacles in the way of the team's mission, arousing the suspicions of Burnham and Tyler.

Meanwhile, far away, L'Rell has been tasked by Kol with interrogating the captured Admiral Cornwell, but confesses to the human that she is ready to defect. Before she can escape with the admiral, however, L'Rell is confronted by Kol, resulting in the apparent death of Cornwell and punishment for L'Rell.

On Pahvo, Burnham manages to retune the transmitter after Tyler tricks a recalcitrant Saru. The *Discovery* crew believes it's mission accomplished – until the planet suddenly sends a new signal, drawing the attention of the Klingons to their location…

(Previous spread)

01 Michael Burnham on the planet Pahvo.

02 Tyler, Burnham, and Saru: lost in the woods.

MARY CHIEFFO
L'Rell

"L'Rell with Cornwell – that's one of my favorite relationships L'Rell has on the show. Of course, there's the Tyler relationship – but I just think there's a real respect [between L'Rell and Cornwell] in that there's a whole first chunk where they were kind of scoping each other out, and Cornwell really proves to L'Rell that she's smart. Cornwell gets that L'Rell is not like all the other Klingons, and L'Rell respects that."

JAMES MACKINNON
Dept. Head Prosthetic and Special FX Make-up

"The look of [Lieutenant Commander] Airiam was difficult to realize because we're mixing silicone with a hard surface – a 3D-printed helmet, ears… We did a test in Toronto – I got the pieces, and was trying to figure out how to get them to be perfectly lined up with each other so it doesn't look like we've slipped a helmet on – that it's all one unit. It started out as taking four and a half hours to do the make-up and we got it down

05

06

to two and a half. Similarly, Doug Jones' Saru make-up initially took three hours and I got it down to one hour and 45 minutes."

GLENN HETRICK
Prosthetic and Special FX Make-up
"Finding Saru, the character, was probably the biggest journey for us as a creative team. He originally looked nothing like the current version! There was a whole separate version of him that almost made it to screen, and it all changed very close to when we started shooting. One of the driving forces to change that original look was that you lost Doug, and when you have a creature-suit performer of that top level, you need to let Doug act through the make-up.

"So we went much more minimal, and got Saru down to something that really facilitates Doug's performance and his ability to emote and create empathy, more so than a lot of make-up. But that was a real challenge – when you're working for months on one look, and then suddenly you're doing something completely different. That's tough." ⋏

03 Saru recovers in sickbay from his Pahvo experience.

04 Into the forest they go...

05 Tilly confronts Stamets over his odd, mycelial-influenced behavior.

06 Lorca and Burnham are alarmed by Pahvo's new signal.

INTO THE FOREST I GO

01

SEASON 1, EPISODE 9

First aired:
November 12, 2017
Writers: Bo Yeon Kim &
Erika Lippoldt
Director: Chris Byrne

CAST

Sonequa Martin-Green:
Michael Burnham
Doug Jones:
Commander Saru
Shazad Latif:
Lieutenant Ash Tyler
Anthony Rapp:
Lieutenant Paul Stamets
Mary Wiseman:
Cadet Sylvia Tilly
Jason Isaacs:
Captain Gabriel Lorca
Jayne Brook: Admiral
Katrina Cornwell
Mary Chieffo: L'Rell
Wilson Cruz:
Doctor Hugh Culber
Kenneth Mitchell: Kol
Conrad Coates:
Admiral Terral
Emily Coutts:
Lieutenant Keyla Detmer
Patrick Kwok-Choon:
Lieutenant Rhys
Sara Mitich: Lieutenant
Commander Airiam
Oyin Oladejo: Lieutenant
Joann Owosekun

SYNOPSIS

With the Pahvo plan in tatters, and the planet in danger following the arrival of Kol's Sarcophagus ship, *Discovery* stands as the world's sole line of defense.

In search of a way of cracking the Klingons' cloaking tech, Captain Lorca finds a solution in the shape of the spore drive. But there's a problem: with every jump he makes, Paul Stamets' mind becomes ever more scrambled, leaving him fearing for his sanity – and to map the dimensions of the cloaked Sarcophagus ship, 133 jumps in rapid succession are called for. Appealing to the explorer in Stamets, with the promise of new frontiers once the war is won, Lorca brings the engineer on board – much to the professional and personal chagrin of Stamets' partner, Doctor Hugh Culber.

As part of the plan, Michael Burnham – the only crew member who has been on the

> "You showed me this invention could take us to places we never dreamed we could reach."
>
> **GABRIEL LORCA
> TO PAUL STAMETS**

Sarcophagus ship – beams aboard the enemy vessel with Ash Tyler in order to position a device to triangulate the spore drive data. Unexpectedly, they find Admiral Cornwell, injured but still alive. They're about to rescue her when L'Rell interrupts, triggering a PTSD attack in Tyler, who had apparently been tortured by L'Rell during his previous imprisonment.

Left to complete the mission alone, Burnham heads to the bridge and activates the tracking device, before engaging in desperate hand-to-hand combat with Kol. She almost gets the best of him, but as *Discovery* completes its data-mining task, she's beamed aboard to safety, along with Tyler, Cornwell... and L'Rell. The Klingon cloak negated, *Discovery* fires upon the Sarcophagus ship, destroying it in a blazing fireball.

A triumphant Lorca convinces Stamets to make one last jump "home"... but possibly due to Lorca's interference, that's not where they end up.

(Previous spread)

01 Cadet Sylvia Tilly keeps the spore drive canisters coming.

02 A tender moment for Culber and Stamets, as the latter prepares to make one last spore drive jump.

WILSON CRUZ
Hugh Culber

"From the very beginning, if we go back to where we first meet Doctor Culber, there was always some tension there between the captain and Culber. Culber came onto this ship, just like everyone else, because it was a science vessel. And suddenly we are at war, and Lorca is putting Culber's lover in direct danger – and for no good reason as far as he can tell, which, as a doctor, is incredibly concerning. [Paul is] being used as a guinea pig; they have no idea what the effects of this are gonna be on him.

"Her name was L'Rell. She's the reason I've had nightmares, every night since the day Captain Lorca and I fled her ship."

ASH TYLER

"[Lorca] is the cause of a lot of angst and stress for my character, and Culber doesn't really see him caring very much about the stresses that he's putting Paul through. So for those reasons, Culber isn't thrilled, and I think he is concerned about where this captain is taking them, and what he's doing. Maybe he's a little too smart for his own good, this Doctor Culber."

TAMARA DEVERELL
Production Designer

"As soon as I get even a kernel of knowledge of what's coming up, I'm working on it myself. I can't wait for scripts, I can't wait for outlines even; if the writers say, 'Oh we're gonna go to such-and-such planet in episode whatever,' I have to start working on it.

03

"And then I'll draw certain people in. We're a very busy art department so some people are working on things that are shooting the next day still, and then I might have three art directors that are supervising, and two that do odds and evens in terms of the episodics, so we're always leapfrogging. And then I'll have a couple of set designers, and always the illustrators are the first to start.

"So concept illustration comes first, and I have a bunch of different people that I work with, some in the office, some out. Our graphic designers also, in a pinch, will do set illustration if I need it. We're just lucky, blessed with a lot of talent!" ⋀

03 Burnham aboard the Sarcophagus ship.

04 Lorca asks Stamets for the impossible: 133 spore drive jumps.

05 Tense times on the *Discovery* bridge.

06 Tyler in the throes of a traumatic flashback aboard the Sarcophagus vessel.

VOYAGE OF DISCOVERY

As much as *Star Trek: Discovery* Season 1 is about twists, turns, and shocks, it's also about revelations of a different kind: those smaller but no less important discoveries that the characters make about themselves and which allow them to grow and develop across the season. None more so than Cadet Sylvia Tilly, whose optimism and humor have made her a fan favorite, and whose voyage through Season 1 was as revelatory for her as it was for the actor who plays her, Mary Wiseman.

Star Trek: Discovery Companion: Early on, some viewers found Sylvia Tilly's enthusiasm and exuberance annoying. We'd maintain she was actually a breath of fresh air. What was your take on Tilly's energy, and why it was essential to the U.S.S. Discovery crew and their mission?
I love Tilly. I agree that she's a breath of fresh air. It's refreshing to have someone who has the same enthusiasm as the fans do watching [the show]. I think Tilly doesn't need to play it cool. She's very comfortable being herself. She wears her passion and heart on her sleeve. I love people like that. I understand why people would think she's grating, but like all people, you have to get to know them before you make a snap judgement.

01 Cadet Sylvia Tilly with tricorder at the ready.

Arguably, Tilly displayed the greatest potential for growth. What were some of the early discussions you had with the producers about where Tilly would start and her journey through Season 1?
What we talked about most was just how green Tilly is. She got fast-tracked onto the ship. Really, from our frame of mind, she's still in college. She's still growing and learning a lot. She's thrust into this situation where she has to become an adult quickly. That allows a lot of potential for growth.

When you are on a starship for Starfleet, you will come across situations that are hard and test you, and test your character. That makes you grow up very quickly and that is what is happening to her. I feel really lucky that they put me

in a lot of tricky situations where Tilly had to show her mettle.

As you mentioned, Tilly is a little bit green. Did she always have something to prove?
Tilly knows what her skillset is. She's the best theoretical engineer on the ship, right off the bat, right when you need her. Tilly's concern was being able to fit in and having connections with the people around her and feeling that love and respect. When she meets Burnham, Tilly is so excited to have someone who kinda has to be her friend. That's the journey she's on: creating these relationships and proving that she's trustworthy and will have your back if you get into trouble. I think she knew

02

more about her technical skills than she did about being a member of a crew and being someone people could fall back on.

The dialogue and bursts of humor that Tilly gets are really fun for me as an actor. That's a place I really like to live. For Tilly, it gives me some clues into who she is. I think she is someone who wants to make people happy and really cares about people and is really honest in the moment. Sometimes when people blurt out their most honest feelings, it's kind of funny. For me, it made her loveable. Tilly speaks from the heart, even when it's misguided, like when she drops the F-bomb and the dammits.

What do you think are some of Tilly's most admirable qualities?
She really leads with her heart. You were saying at the beginning how some viewers find Tilly annoying. I can't imagine that's the first time Tilly encountered that. She's probably had experiences in her life where she wasn't fitting in or had troubles making friends. My personal take on it is she leads with compassion because that's how she wants

02 Tilly, Burnham, Tyler, and Lorca discuss their parallel universe predicament in "Despite Yourself."

03 Tilly – in her Killy uniform – with Saru and a comatose Stamets – both of whom she has forged strong bonds with. ("The Wolf Inside")

04 Burnham gets a frosty reception from Tilly in "Context Is for Kings."

to be treated. I think when she looks at tough situations, she makes choices that are based on kindness. That's something I love about her and I continue to learn from her. That's also very, very *Star Trek*, leading with love.

Across Season 1, Tilly interacted with a lot of the crew, but forged strong bonds with three of them in particular. Tell us about her relationships with Michael Burnham, Saru, and Paul Stamets.
The touchstone for me was Burnham, because that was her first entrance point into the deeper world of this ship, the deeper ongoings into this war and ongoings into the Federation and Starfleet. Having a friend like Burnham was so important to her — someone in a time of war who you can be soft with and who you can try and help, and be helped by, through kindness and warmth and communication. That was so important to her journey. Some of that also helped Burnham; that softness and vulnerability and being able to talk and express your feelings. They really helped each other get to a different place in their lives.

04

03

With Stamets, Tilly has this sort of unrelenting positivity and optimism. She kept battering at him with that until he finally caved. There's moments in the show where they get to see each other in a different way and their relationship was able to transform through that. That affected what they were able to do with their science and engineering, because they were open to each other in a different way.

With Saru, here's a high officer on the ship. Being able to stand up to him, and work with him, feeling like an equal with him, changed the way she saw herself. In that moment, I don't think she felt like a cadet. She felt like a peer. In turn, Saru treated her like that and has really encouraged her and had a really big part in her entrance into the Command Training Program. That's a transformational episode also.

> "Tilly speaks from the heart, even when it's misguided, like when she drops the F-bomb."
>
> **MARY WISEMAN**

Do you think Tilly has learned anything from Captain Lorca?
I don't think she's learned from captains. Lorca is an interesting study, but it didn't work out that way. She's learning from bad and good. She learned from Mirror Georgiou in their brief time with each other. She's also learning from Burnham. And, she's watching Burnham grow, watching Saru grow, and watching Stamets grow. Seeing them, again and again, choose to do the right thing – the ethical thing – and to embody the spirit of Starfleet and not just a commander on high – she's learning from Saru, Burnham, and Stamets.

Which were some of your favorite episodes to film?
I loved when she found out about Captain Killy. That was a fun episode

to shoot and there was a lot of comedy. That was a genuine blast. And, I loved the last episode. I thought it was so much fun to go down to another planet, to this marketplace, where everyone is out of their element and on their guard. I got to do some espionage. Those two episodes were a ball. Jonathan Frakes and Akiva Goldman directed those episodes.

> ## "I loved the Mirror costume. It was all black leather and gold-plated armor. It was very sexy and sort of dominatrix-y."
> **MARY WISEMAN**

How happy were you with where the season finale left Tilly and what it means for her moving forward?
I'm so psyched about where the season finale left Tilly. She's on the Command Training Program, which is exactly where she should be. She's on the bridge. She's going to learn from the best of the best. She's going to be right in the action. She's right where she needs to be to get where she needs to go.

Looking at the second half of the season, viewers were introduced to the Mirror Universe. That in turn introduced us to Captain Killy. What was that like to play?
It was so much fun. You have her impersonating someone who was almost a polar opposite of herself and showing little glimpses of what's inside her beyond what we've already seen. You see she can project power and confidence and that she can wield a terrifying blood thirstiness when necessary. You get to see her shadow self, and it fills her out for the audience – and it filled her out for me a bit.

What was your impression of her costume, and how did it help you get into character?
I loved the Mirror costume. It was all black leather and gold-plated armor. It was very sexy and sort of dominatrix-y. For me, it gave me that sharp-toothedness that Captain Killy had, and the big, broad, triangular armor… It makes you feel like a gladiator or a warrior. It's always helpful when the costume informs the person inside it, which our costume designer Gersha [Phillips] does really well.

STAR TREK
GENERATIONS

How did you find working with Jonathan Frakes, director of Episode 10, "Despite Yourself," and of course veteran of *Star Trek: The Next Generation*?

It's so nice. He comes to it with so much compassion and stories of his time on *Next Generation*. He was an actor before, so he really gets it and treats everyone with kindness and respect. He's such a bright light. We are always having fun. He's a genuinely lovely person and a great director.

Tell us about that iconic moment of sitting in the captain's chair as Captain Killy. How did you approach it, and how did it affect Tilly?

Jonathan Frakes pulled me aside and was like, "Can you just take that moment to really sit there, to really take in being in the captain's chair. And, even though this moment is really scary for you, enjoy it a little bit." I thought that note was a watershed moment for the character. That is a moment she will never forget for the rest of her life.

05

06

> ## "Tilly knew more about her technical skills than she did about being a member of a crew and someone people could fall back on."
>
> **MARY WISEMAN**

05 "Captain Killy" in the big chair in "Despite Yourself," with Burnham, Lorca, and the rest of the bridge crew playing along.

06 Tilly in disguise once more, this time on Qo'noS in "Will You Take My Hand?"

Behind the scenes, we have created a narrative about hair among women. You don't often see curly-haired or natural-haired heroines or lead actresses. That's something we played with: when someone straightens their hair, or someone tries to make their hair look different than it naturally is, is that a way of not really embracing who they really are? Maybe this woman in the Mirror Universe, who wants to project this power and cutthroatedness, maybe she feels she needs to alter herself in order to project that. But, back home in Starfleet on the *Discovery*, we are comfortable being ourselves and letting that real power shine through.

Upon reflection, do you think that whole adventure – and assuming the role of Captain Killy – proved to be a turning point for Tilly?

I think Tilly had that abstract notion of, "I want to be a captain one day. I want to achieve all these dreams and be in this place." Taking on the persona of Captain Killy gave her a little window into that. She got to sit in the captain's chair. She got to command the people on the bridge. And, she got to engage with other ships. Tilly was self-actualized in that moment. Even though she was putting something on, Tilly still got to embody that for a second. She got a glimpse into what that really means. It's not abstract any more.

More importantly, other people on the ship got to see what she could do. That reinforced her confidence and belief and has affected her pretty deeply.

Ultimately, Tilly proved a key player in getting the crew home...

I was so excited. The student became the teacher. You see the maturation and growth of Stamets and her relationship. He trusts her, and he trusts her ideas and her problem-solving abilities. It felt like a moment of her both having the confidence to voice her ideas and take on such a big project, and also, the crew's ability to trust her in that role.

Because the stakes are high. She had to have the confidence. What mattered wasn't her role on the ship. What mattered was bringing Stamets back. Those moments are so important to people's growth – when you are challenged and when you think everything is impossible, and you find a way through. That's how you become an adult. That's what is happening with her. That's her journey. ʌ

DESPITE
YOURSELF

First aired: January 7, 2018
Writer: Sean Cochran
Director: Jonathan Frakes

CAST

Sonequa Martin-Green:
Michael Burnham
Doug Jones:
Commander Saru
Shazad Latif:
Lieutenant Ash Tyler
Anthony Rapp:
Lieutenant Paul Stamets
Mary Wiseman:
Cadet Sylvia Tilly
Jason Isaacs:
Captain Gabriel Lorca
Wilson Cruz:
Doctor Hugh Culber
Mary Chieffo: L'Rell
Sam Vartholomeos:
Mirror Danby Connor
Emily Coutts: Lieutenant
Keyla Detmer/Mirror
Keyla Detmer
Patrick Kwok-Choon:
Lieutenant Rhys
Sara Mitich: Lieutenant
Commander Airiam
Ali Momen:
Kamran Grant
Oyin Oladejo: Lieutenant
Joann Owosekun
Ronnie Rowe Jr.:
Lieutenant R. A. Bryce
Chris Violette:
Britch Weeton
Romaine Waite:
Troy Januzzi

02

SYNOPSIS

With the *U.S.S. Discovery*'s position unknown following Lieutenant Stamets' disastrous final spore drive jump, Michael Burnham's scans indicate that nearby wreckage originates from a different quantum universe. Meanwhile, in the brig, Ash Tyler speaks Klingon to the captive L'Rell, who expresses confusion at Tyler's inability to remember his *other* name. Who could he possibly be…?

Analyzing a salvaged data core, Burnham determines that *Discovery* has traveled to a parallel reality ruled by xenophobic Terrans. The *U.S.S. Defiant* also arrived here at some point, so Burnham plans to steal information about the *Defiant*'s journey from the *I.S.S. Shenzhou*, which

> "Destiny didn't get me out of prison, Captain. You did that."
>
> **MICHAEL BURNHAM TO GABRIEL LORCA**

this reality's Burnham was formerly captain of.

Seemingly remarkably well-prepared for his ship's unexpected detour, Captain Lorca maintains that the *Discovery* crew must think and act like Terrans in order to survive these hostile environs. That directive is tested to the extreme when Cadet Tilly is forced to assume command of *Discovery* in order to sustain the ruse, much to her discomfort.

In a shocking turn of events, Tyler murders Doctor Culber to prevent the doctor from quarantining him. His crime yet to be discovered, Tyler vows to protect Burnham as she takes command of the *Shenzhou* (an action that entails her killing the current captain of the *Shenzhou*, Danby Connor, who attacks her in the turbolift). But can he truly be trusted…?

(Previous spread)

01 Burnham shares a tender moment with Tyler, unaware that he has committed a terrible crime.

02 Saru, Burnham, and Lorca realize they are in a parallel universe.

GRETCHEN J. BERG
Executive Producer

"One of the opportunities of being on a streaming format is that we were able to explore storylines at length. This storyline came out of the characters of L'Rell and Tyler and how they knew each other, and the story of being on that prison ship, and making sure that it made sense as we looked back at their characters. That was just an aspect of what the relationship was between Voq and L'Rell, and Tyler and L'Rell, and being able to realize that there was a sexual aspect between the two of them.

"It was so interesting to be able to talk about it with the actors – Shazad [Latif – Tyler/Voq] and

> "You know what we did. We did it together. So many things... You have such appetites..."
>
> **L'RELL TO ASH TYLER**

also Mary [Chieffo – L'Rell], who's so fantastic – and to entrust them and have them trust us, in order to tell that story. It's something that we've never really been able to go into that sort of depth with before – it's a very specific relationship dynamic. I was really proud of how it was handled by everybody."

MARY CHIEFFO
L'Rell

"It was always fun to get a new script, because I never quite knew what they were gonna do! The whole Tyler plot was so complex and interesting. I remember turning to Sonequa [Martin-Green] around Episode 10, and saying, 'Do you know

where this is all gonna go…?' And she was like, 'I don't know…' And I was like, 'Well, I respect you!'

"More of a surprising moment off screen was actually that scene [in the brig between L'Rell and Tyler] in Episode 10. Sonequa and Jason [Isaacs – Lorca] happened to be on set for the next scene, and Shazad and I didn't know, so for most of his close-ups they were watching us do the scene over and over again. It was complex and crazy, and then midway through, Sonequa comes in, and she's crying, and she's like, 'You guys!' It's a testament to how amazing she is; she was just so thrilled with what she was seeing, and she could see the complexity of what was going on between these characters, and she said it informed her so much. Shazad and Sonequa and I had this bizarre hug, with me in the jail suit…

"And then later on, Jason was like [in British accent], 'It was very good.'" [Laughs]

"A big journey for me, too, was embracing the fact that Klingons are innately sensual creatures, in a way that the humans aren't. To me that was part of what made them beautifully alien, and part of what I was able to justify, certainly in the scene in 'Despite Yourself,' that Jonathan Frakes directed so amazingly. That scene was so complex, and Shazad and I were like, 'We don't want this to just be some creepy Hannibal Lecter sort of situation.' For me, L'Rell is using her sensuality – she is not a puritan. She has not been taught to have a certain shame around her sensuality; she is using that because that's love, also.

"For her, that connection with Voq is not just carnal, it's pure and it's genuine. The way she navigates it is more alien than human. That's a beautiful gift of science fiction – that you can explore these themes in a slightly different way than you would if it was just two humans interacting. But it's interesting to see, too, that her empowerment by that is misconstrued by the humans." ⋀

03 With Lorca as her prisoner, Burnham beams to the *I.S.S. Shenzhou* – to be met by Danby Connor.

04 Tilly and Culber discuss the prognosis for Stamets.

05 An intense moment, as Tyler confronts L'Rell in the *Discovery* brig.

06 Tilly in disguise as the Mirror Universe's Captain "Killy."

THE WOLF INSIDE

SEASON 1, EPISODE 11

First aired:
January 14, 2018
Writer: Lisa Randolph
Director: TJ Scott

CAST

Sonequa Martin-Green:
Michael Burnham
Doug Jones:
Commander Saru/
Mirror Saru
Shazad Latif: Lieutenant
Ash Tyler/Mirror Voq
Anthony Rapp:
Lieutenant Paul Stamets/
Mirror Paul Stamets
Mary Wiseman:
Cadet Sylvia Tilly
Jason Isaacs:
Captain Gabriel Lorca
Wilson Cruz:
Doctor Hugh Culber
James Frain: Mirror Sarek
Michelle Yeoh:
Mirror Emperor
Philippa Georgiou
Emily Coutts:
Lieutenant Keyla Detmer
Riley Gilchrist: Shukar
Devon MacDonald:
Service Engineer
Ali Momen:
Kamran Grant
Dwain Murphy:
Captain Maddox
Chris Violette:
Britch Weeton
Romaine Waite:
Troy Januzzi

01

SYNOPSIS

As Michael Burnham familiarizes herself with her surroundings aboard the *I.S.S. Shenzhou*, back on *Discovery* Commander Saru permits Cadet Tilly to treat Paul Stamets – still in a coma following the jump that brought the ship to the Mirror Universe – with a spore-based procedure. Deriving an odd confidence from her brief tenure as "Captain Killy," rather than being emboldened by Killy's rank, Tilly strives to demonstrate she bears no resemblance to her genocidal parallel.

Burnham chooses to meet with the leader of a group of rebels fighting the Terran Empire, in order to learn how he united Klingons with other races. That commander turns out to be

> "Sometimes the end justifies terrible means."
> **GABRIEL LORCA**

the Mirror version of Voq, whose words provoke Tyler into a frenzied but failed assault on the Klingon commander. Later, Burnham confronts Tyler and learns that her lover is, in fact, the Voq of her universe, surgically altered and imprinted with Tyler's memories.

As Stamets regains consciousness within the mycelial network and meets his alternate reality counterpart, on the *Shenzhou* Burnham executes Voq/Tyler in the required Terran manner: by beaming him into space. However, it is a ploy that allows *Discovery* to rescue the spy – along with the stolen *U.S.S. Defiant* data Burnham has secreted on him.

Then the *Shenzhou* receives a hail from *Emperor* Philippa Georgiou…

(Previous spread)

01 Mirror Voq with his Terran rebellion lieutenants.

02 Michael Burnham with the Mirror version of her father, Sarek.

GERSHA PHILLIPS
Costume Designer

"When we did the Terran uniform plated arms, they would snap off all the time… This is the thing about designing: you're given the impetus from the story, and then you draw it out and you come up with this really great design; and then you have to bring it into reality, which is a whole other ballgame.

"When it's written, we get an outline – it's very vague and very brief – and then the story comes out and it's way more complicated, there are more stunts involved, and the story has evolved into something else; and you're like, 'Wow, I didn't plan on *that* being used for *that*!'"

MARIO MOREIRA
Property Master

"I think we had already set the bar so high for ourselves in terms of designing this world and creating this world, and then the Mirror Universe landed in front of us. We were like, 'These guys are military, they like their bling, they like to show their achievements – we've really gotta push the envelope here with what we're doing and really nail it.' And I think we did. I think it was pretty successful, the whole look of it."

TAMARA DEVERELL
Production Designer

"When we went to the rebel planet in Episode 11, we did it right outside the studio in the parking

> "Can you hide your heart? Can you bury your decency? Can you continue to pretend to be one of them? Even as, little by little, it kills the person you really are."
>
> **MICHAEL BURNHAM**

03

03 Tyler loses it and attacks Mirror Voq – or rather, the Mirror version of himself!

04 Captain Lorca, consigned to the agonizers.

05 Burnham and Tyler make their entrance at the rebellion meeting.

06 A Mirror Universe Andorian.

lot, the gravel lot. We wanted to do it elsewhere; we had done part of it in a quarry, where we were setting off bombs and stuff, and it looked very alien; but it was just a big deal to take such a big group of people, the crew, out to a quarry.

"So I said, 'Look, there's that gravel lot over there; with some help from VFX in the wide shots, let's just do our camp encampment there.' Which felt very original series; it felt kind of like what they might have done, just going out to the backyard and shooting a scene. It looked great. But they didn't have the effects then, so you kind of got what you got." ⋀

VAULTING AMBITION

SEASON 1, EPISODE 12

First aired:
January 21, 2018
Writer: Jordon Nardino
Director:
Hanelle M. Culpepper

CAST

Sonequa Martin-Green: Michael Burnham
Doug Jones: Commander Saru
Shazad Latif: Lieutenant Ash Tyler
Anthony Rapp: Lieutenant Paul Stamets/Mirror Paul Stamets
Mary Wiseman: Cadet Sylvia Tilly
Jason Isaacs: Captain Gabriel Lorca
Michelle Yeoh: Mirror Emperor Philippa Georgiou
Mary Chieffo: L'Rell
Wilson Cruz: Doctor Hugh Culber
Jeremy Crittenden: Lord Eling
Raven Dauda: Doctor Pollard
Billy MacLellan: Barlow
Dwain Murphy: Captain Maddox

SYNOPSIS

Arriving on Emperor Georgiou's gargantuan flagship, the *I.S.S. Charon*, Michael Burnham learns from the Terran tyrant that in this universe, Georgiou raised her version of Burnham as a daughter. Furthermore, it appears that Georgiou uncovered a plot by her Burnham and Gabriel Lorca to steal her throne. To avoid execution, Burnham unveils her true identity, agreeing to supply information on spore drive technology in exchange for *Discovery*'s freedom.

Back on *Discovery*, Saru recruits a reluctant L'Rell to perform a procedure to remove Voq's consciousness from Voq/Ash Tyler's body,

> "Logic tells me she's not the woman that I betrayed. But this feels like a reckoning."
>
> **MICHAEL BURNHAM**

thus alleviating his suffering. Meanwhile, in the mycelial network, Paul Stamets encounters a vision of his murdered lover, Hugh Culber. The late doctor explains the ramifications of the dying network, and guides Paul on the path to awakening, with the aid of a piece of Kasseelian opera that's always been central to their relationship.

On the *Charon*, Emperor Georgiou describes Lorca's counterpart as Mirror Burnham's manipulative father figure… and lover. The tale, along with the revelation that Terrans share an innate photosensitivity – in common with Captain Lorca – leads Burnham to a terrible realization: her Lorca has been *Mirror* Lorca all along.

(Previous spread)

01 Emperor Georgiou certainly knows how to make an entrance.

02 Tilly and Saru fret about Paul Stamets.

GRETCHEN J. BERG
Executive Producer

"We knew some of the season's story reveals from the beginning, but it was a case where reveals begat reveals begat reveals."

AARON HARBERTS
Executive Producer

"Often Gretchen and I will start thinking, 'Oh, this story is gonna take a whole season to reveal.' And then we'd think, 'Well, why not?' You can get good stuff out of it. As long as the reveal was a game-changer, we would do it. We wouldn't create twists just to do a twist. Georgiou dies – it has a ripple effect through the entire season; Lorca is revealed to be Mirror Lorca – that affects how you view the series when you watch it a second time.

"If it was ever something that would knock our characters for a loop, we were excited to do it. Culber's death, for example – it's one of many things that were very baked into the season."

05

06

TAMARA DEVERELL
Production Designer

"Georgiou's Terran Empire ship was a lot of work. We had to do it super fast – because we were into the episodic time frame, which is super fast – so I had to come up with something really big and awesome really quickly! So I said, 'Okay, we're gonna go brutalist, kind of crazy' – it's brutalist architecture, which is not canon. So we did something different, which was also interesting.

"And then creating the ship itself, we had to create something that was bigger and meaner than anything we'd ever seen on *Star Trek*. That was challenging and exciting... Even though the ship is all VFX, we had to do the design work. I had this idea that because it was so big, I personally couldn't wrap my head around it – I felt

> "It's never goodbye. Isn't that what you've been trying to teach all of us? Nothing in here is ever truly gone. I believe in you, Paul. I love you."
>
> **HUGH CULBER**

that it needed its own power source. So I said to the writers, 'Can I put a sun in it? Like it's got its own mini sun, that's running the whole thing, that they're drawing energy from.' And then they took that and they made it into the mycelial sun. So that was a really interesting moment of laying the design, and then the story on top of it, and they grew out of each other.

"That was probably the most exciting thing. That and Jonathan Frakes coming in and going: 'There's roofs?!' on our sets. I guess on *Next Gen* they didn't have ceilings. So I go, 'Jonathan, they're called ceilings, not roofs.' 'No, they're roofs! You've got roofs everywhere!' He was just so delighted and excited at seeing the next generation of *Star Trek* – the new next generation." ⌃

03 Posing as her own Mirror counterpart, Michael Burnham meets the emperor.

04 Lorca on the receiving end of some rough treatment... shortly before doling some out himself.

05 All hail Emperor Georgiou.

06 The cunning, ruthless Mirror Georgiou.

WHAT'S PAST IS PROLOGUE

SEASON 1, EPISODE 13

First aired:
January 28, 2018
Writer: Ted Sullivan
Director:
Olatunde Osunsanmi

CAST

Sonequa Martin-Green:
Michael Burnham
Doug Jones:
Commander Saru
Shazad Latif:
Lieutenant Ash Tyler
Anthony Rapp:
Lieutenant Paul Stamets/
Mirror Paul Stamets
Mary Wiseman:
Cadet Sylvia Tilly
Jason Isaacs:
Captain Gabriel Lorca
Michelle Yeoh:
Mirror Emperor
Philippa Georgiou
Rekha Sharma:
Mirror Ellen Landry
Emily Coutts:
Lieutenant Keyla Detmer
Jeremy Crittenden:
Lord Eling
Patrick Kwok-Choon:
Lieutenant Rhys
Sara Mitich: Lieutenant
Commander Airiam
Ali Momen:
Kamran Grant
Oyin Oladejo: Lieutenant
Joann Owosekun/Mirror
Joann Owosekun
Ronnie Rowe Jr.:
Lieutenant R. A. Bryce

01

SYNOPSIS

Now uncovered as the Mirror Universe Gabriel Lorca – having switched places with his counterpart during a transporter incident back when each commanded their respective *U.S.S./I.S.S. Buran*s – the erstwhile captain of the *Discovery* initiates a rebellion. Freeing his followers from the agony booths aboard the *I.S.S. Charon*, he leads them in an all-out assault on Emperor Georgiou and her forces.

Meanwhile, on *Discovery*, a revived Paul Stamets discovers that the central orb powering the *Charon* is the cause of the mycelial network's degradation, and must be destroyed. As *Discovery*'s de facto captain, Saru steps up to the mark, rallying his crew with a rousing speech in the face of overwhelming odds.

On the *Charon*, Lorca's forces secure the flagship, at the cost of many Terrans' lives, while Michael Burnham enlists a defeated Georgiou to help deactivate the power core's shields. The two infiltrate the throne room, where the ensuing fight concludes with an impaled Lorca plummeting into the ship's reactor.

Warping into the fray, *Discovery* rescues Burnham – along with an unwilling Georgiou, grabbed by Burnham as she's beamed to safety – and destroys the central orb. Stamets navigates the ship along the mycelial shockwave and brings the crew home – nine months into a future where the Klingons are winning the war...

> "The Federation is a social experiment, doomed to failure."
> **GABRIEL LORCA**

> "I was just thinking about everyone who's ever said that victory felt empty when it was attained. What a bunch of idiots they were."
>
> **GABRIEL LORCA**

AARON HARBERTS
Executive Producer

"How did we get through this, and how did we manage to pull this all together? It's nothing short of a miracle really, because we were so shot out of a cannon.

"But what it did allow us to do was have a unity of vision. We really did lock arms and say, 'This is what we're doing, there's no room for doubt. This is how it's going,' and you plough through it. So, with some of the reveals we pulled things [forward]…

"Another thing that happened was we were initially only supposed to do 13 [episodes]. And then as episodes started coming in and the network started getting more excited, they added two more, and that shifted our storytelling quite a bit.

We would have ended, probably, with the Mirror Universe and getting home. But then we had more to do. So, it was fun. It was fun to watch people get surprised."

GERSHA PHILLIPS
Costume Designer

"I remember the throne room scene that day; looking at that scene on the camera, it was beautiful to watch: Michelle Yeoh coming down the stairs – the whole thing was just: *wow*. And trying to get the sword on her [*laughs*], because it was really big and she's quite petite… I had two ideas for the jacket; one was to do a tail thing that went in the back, and I should have stuck with that, I feel. But she needed the sword to be there, it had to be on the outside."

(Previous spread)

01 Face to face with the manipulative Mirror Lorca.

02 Michael Burnham, phaser at the ready, in the throne room.

03

MARIO MOREIRA
Property Master

"The sword was fun! To get the sword into production, we quickly went to one of my sword-builders and he made a mock-up of it. We had to try it on Michelle, because she is petite, and she is also quite a proficient weapons master. I had to get it into production the next day, so I raced over to the airport, because she had been off on a trip. I called her, and I rushed to the airport, wrapped the sword in a towel, ran into the airport, ran to security, and was like, 'Hi, I don't wanna alarm you, but I'm a props master with a TV show, and I have a sword in here, and I have to try it on this actor who's arriving.' And without blinking, they were like, 'Oh we have this private boardroom you could use' – as if someone runs in with a sword every day!" ⋀

03 Emperor Georgiou leads her troops into battle against Lorca's forces.

04 Lorca caresses Georgiou's sword as he savors his triumph.

05 Burnham in action aboard the *Charon*.

06 Mirror Stamets at the mercy of Mirror Landry.

CREATURE COORDINATOR

As *Star Trek: Discovery*'s Prosthetic and Special Make-up FX Department Head, James MacKinnon is on the front line in Toronto, where the show is filmed. A *Trek* veteran, it's his responsibility to oversee the application of the make-up and prosthetics created by Glenn Hetrick and Neville Page in LA – no easy task in a first season boasting a multitude of Klingons and a certain Kelpien first officer...

01

B ack in the mid-1960s, legendary beauty make-up artist Fred Phillips took on an ambitious new sci-fi TV series called *Star Trek*. While Phillips could create a gorgeous Orion Slave Girl or a bunch of swarthy bearded Klingons, prosthetic-based aliens were a bit out of his wheelhouse. It was common for him to ring up his old friend, make-up FX legend John Chambers (who was also making Spock ears for him at $25 a pair), to see if Chambers had a few leftover facial appliances that could be repurposed at the last minute as aliens.

01 Kenneth Mitchell as Kol, one of *Discovery*'s distinctive Klingons.

02 The striking figure of Saru, as played by Doug Jones.

Bizarrely, some of those characters have become iconic over the years, despite the fact that those prosthetic pieces were often cut up or put on upside-down.

Two decades later, Michael Westmore (incidentally, a former Chambers protégé) took on the job of make-up department head on *Star Trek: The Next Generation*. That gig went on for nearly 15 years, encompassing four different TV series, a couple of films, and a ton of Emmy nominations and awards. Most of Westmore's alien designs would end up accepted as canonical characters.

Until more recently, that is. The three films comprising the new *Star*

Trek movie-verse have drastically altered the paradigm in terms of what could be done with alien make-up FX, and that baton has now been handed off to the team of *Star Trek: Discovery*. On the newest *Trek* TV show, the make-up FX have been designed and built by the team at Alchemy FX Studios in Los Angeles, and overseen by prosthetic/special FX make-up department head James MacKinnon in Toronto, where the series is shot.

MacKinnon is no stranger to the *Star Trek* franchise, having worked on *Deep Space Nine*, the 1997 *Starfleet Academy* video game, and two of the

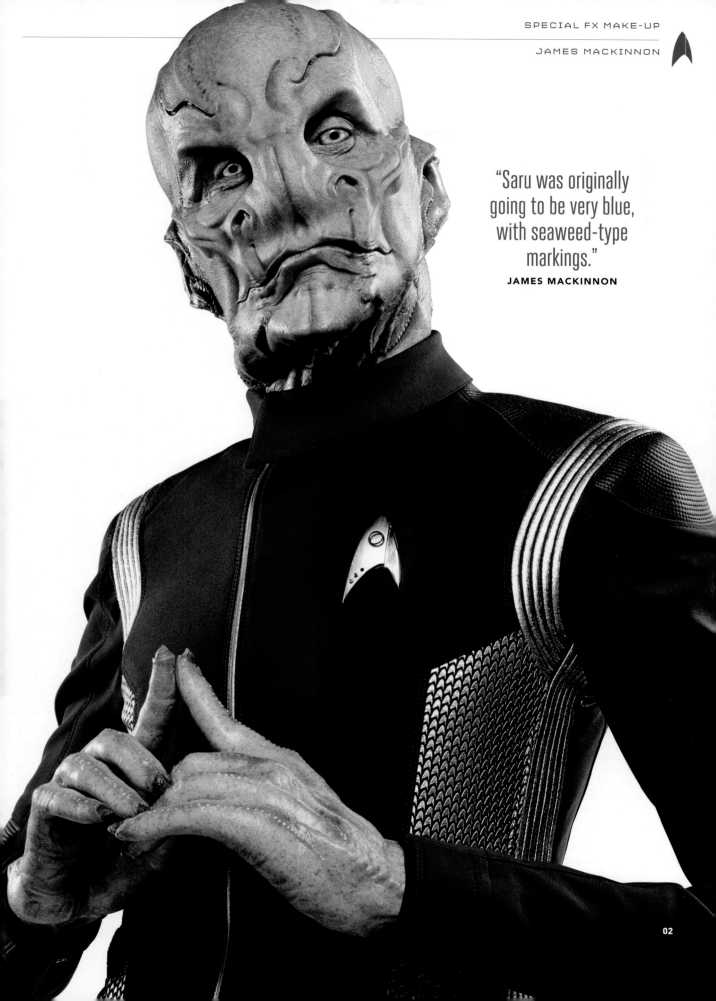

"Saru was originally going to be very blue, with seaweed-type markings."

JAMES MACKINNON

feature films. "I got involved in *Discovery* through two producer friends of mine, Alex Kurtzman and Heather Kadin, with whom I've worked on several shows in the past," he explains. "I worked with Alex all the way back when he was a writer on *Alias*, so I've been with this producing team for many years. They know my work and we all make a great product together."

"At the same time, I've also known [Alchemy chief] Glenn Hetrick for a long time. Glenn said, 'You know the other producers… so this could be a perfect team. You're an amazing department head, and I'm an amazing shop designer, along with [creature designer] Neville Page!' So that's how the team came together.

"At one point, I was still shooting *The Fast and the Furious 8*, and *Discovery* was supposed to start several months sooner than it actually did, so I didn't think I would be finished in time. *Discovery* got pushed back a little on the schedules, so I asked Glenn, 'Is it still happening?' and he said, 'Perfect timing!' So everybody called everybody and Heather Kadin said, 'James has to be on this!' Suddenly we're in Toronto shooting."

CROSS-COUNTRY DISCOVERY

With *Discovery* being shot in Toronto rather than LA, the make-up FX team needed to create a seamless cross-country pipeline where the prosthetics, specialty props, and costume elements could be shipped from Alchemy to Toronto across the border. "I think we already knew the process," reveals MacKinnon, "because I've done this so many times, so between my department head skills and Glenn's shop skills, it all naturally came together.

"What Glenn and I did was sit down together and hash out everything we wanted to do on the show, so everything ran great from the very beginning. We had to make sure everything got shipped to us on time; there was a little worry about that so we asked for six weeks for our prep and build. Of course they never give you that but we were trying to allow enough time for Neville's design work, sculpting, molding, painting, and getting everything to us in time so we could do make-up tests before we started shooting. Sometimes that doesn't always work out and a make-up has to go right to film. But I think our knowledge of the business made this a very smoothly running show."

"We did have to think about the mass production of the Klingons, and how we were going to get 16 sets of prosthetics on set in four hours every morning."

JAMES MACKINNON

One of MacKinnon's biggest challenges during the early days of production was not having access to the large LA talent pool he was used to working with. "I was able to bring Rocky Faulkner and Hugo Villasenor as my two key make-up artists, so they really helped me with all the plates I had spinning at the same time.

"I was able to bring up 11 Los Angeles make-up artists for Episode 1 and 6 for Episode 2. That comfort level really helped me establish the look of the show, because I could say, 'Hey, Eryn Krueger, do this, Mike Mekash, go do this…' and that was really helpful.

"I've got four people who are basically here every day [now], so I feel comfortable enough to say, 'Hey, I'm coming in an hour later tomorrow because of my turnaround, so can you start this make-up for me?' That's a huge thing."

BLUE SARU

MacKinnon's main make-up is Doug Jones, who plays the Kelpien science officer Lieutenant Saru. The character's four-piece prosthetic went through a number of changes before arriving at the final version, including a couple of major color changes. "He was originally going to be very blue, with seaweed-type markings, which looked awesome, but I think the flesh color look is pretty cool too. I still add some marbling to him,

03 Sara Mitich as Airiam, a memorable member of *Discovery*'s bridge crew.

04 Chris Obi as T'Kuvma, leader of House T'Kuvma.

05 Saru in Episode 4, "The Butcher's Knife Cares Not for the Lamb's Cry."

06 A menacing, magnificent Kol.

and maybe add some blue and purple to his temples to make it a bit more translucent-looking, and I'll make his face a bit more crustacean-like. There are also little membranes on his temples, so it was a real learning curve during the early days.

"Doug's make-up also covers his nose, and he had a cold during his first day at work, so his speech was very nasal, and everybody was concerned about his breathing. His nose holes were above his breathing holes, so we thought, 'We can't have this for the rest of the season. He's got to be able to breathe through his nose!'

"So we snipped out a little channel on the back of one of his prosthetics, which went down to his sculpted nose holes. We added a bit of KY in there, so when we glued it down, it didn't attach to the skin. That enabled Doug to breathe, and then I called the shop and said, 'We're going to send you the piece we just used so you can create these little channels in the core when you run the pieces.' That way, the channels would be automatically built in, so Doug would be more com-fortable, and it allowed us to hear his voice instead of a nasal Doug. Those are the kinds of things we worked on together for the benefit of the show and our actor."

COMPLEX KLINGONS

Another alien race that plays a major role in *Discovery* Season 1 are the Klingons, with whom the Federation are embroiled in an intergalactic war. "Our Klingons are very complicated," notes MacKinnon, "and I think Glenn and Neville did an amazing job with the design and creation.

"From the very beginning, we wanted the show to be different from past *Star Trek* TV shows, even though this is only 10 years before Kirk and Spock. The original Klingons had a Fu Manchu goatee and very tan, painted faces, so it's a bit hard to say that time has passed between series, but the producers were always very clear that these are not the movie Klingons.

> "Like the work they did on the original *Star Trek*, these are timeless make-ups. It's stuff that people are going to look at in a few years and say, 'That's great!'"
>
> **JAMES MACKINNON**

"The other cool thing about our show is we're doing different Klingon 'houses.' I want to say there are as many as 24 different houses, and every house is from a different area. Some might have battle wounds; some might have different paint jobs in different colors and different bone structure. And there are different ranks with different-colored costumes, which the color of the make-up betrays as well.

07

MARY CHIEFFO
L'RELL

"James MacKinnon is the make-up man on the ground in Toronto. James and I have spent many hours together. He's cleaned up my drool… In Episode 12, I kept crying and I couldn't blow my nose [because of the Klingon prosthetics], so he kept stuffing tissues up my nose for me – it was really glamorous!"

"We did have to think about the mass production of the Klingons, and how we were going to get 16 sets of prosthetics on set in four hours every morning, so each one is broken down into two or three pieces, maybe four. We're doing a lot of cowls, faces, upper and lower lips, and sometimes a chin. We try to break the mouth apart, because they're speaking a lot and they have those big Klingon teeth in, so we want to get as much facial movement as possible. You definitely don't want a big, static, one-piece silicone face with no movement in it whatsoever.

"Sometimes we'll get an actor who needs a little help, so you have to tell them, 'Hey, if you want to move your eyebrows, you have to move them four times as much to get them to move on the outside!' We also use a couple of beautiful background masks that Glenn and Neville designed, and if the actors underneath are not normally mask or character actors, you've got to say, 'Look to your right or left, but look with your *mask* not with your eyes, because you're still looking around underneath it.'

"Those are the things we have to deal

07 Mary Chieffo as L'Rell of House T'Kuvma and House Mo'Kai.

with, because we want to get as much facial movement as we possibly can, so you need as much life to come out of it in order to compensate for the thickness of the mask. It's very different if you're just doing a thin little silicone appliance, because you wouldn't get the amount of actual depth you need to change that character to get him to look a certain way, especially if it's a Klingon character."

With *Discovery*'s first season done and dusted, MacKinnon – a *Star Trek* veteran and a fan himself – reports he's pleased with the way things have come together so smoothly. "Like the work they did on the original *Star Trek*, these are timeless make-ups," he reflects. "It's stuff that people are going to look at in a few years and say, 'That's great!' We're taking some of the make-ups from the original series and bringing them into the work we're doing today, and I think it's phenomenal, cool stuff. I'm lucky. This job is hard and stressful, but it's also amazing and fun, and while Glenn and I will never be the new Michael Westmores, it's the next step in this universe, so it's cool to be part of something this historic." ᴧ

A Tellarite,
as seen in
Episode 11,
"The Wolf Inside."

THE WAR WITHOUT, THE WAR WITHIN

SEASON 1, EPISODE 14

First aired:
February 4, 2018
Writer: Lisa Randolph
Director: David Solomon

CAST

Sonequa Martin-Green: Michael Burnham
Doug Jones: Commander Saru
Shazad Latif: Lieutenant Ash Tyler
Anthony Rapp: Lieutenant Paul Stamets
Mary Wiseman: Cadet Sylvia Tilly
Michelle Yeoh: Mirror Emperor Philippa Georgiou
Jayne Brook: Admiral Katrina Cornwell
Mary Chieffo: L'Rell
James Frain: Sarek
Emily Coutts: Lieutenant Keyla Detmer
Raven Dauda: Doctor Pollard
Patrick Kwok-Choon: Lieutenant Rhys
Sara Mitich: Lieutenant Commander Airiam
Oyin Oladejo: Lieutenant Joann Owosekun
Ronnie Rowe Jr.: Lieutenant R. A. Bryce

SYNOPSIS

"There is irony here, of course. The man you fell in love with was a Klingon... There is also grace. For what greater source of peace exists than our ability to love our enemy."

SAREK TO MICHAEL BURNHAM

No sooner have the crew of *Discovery* returned to their own universe, than Admiral Cornwell and Sarek board the starship in a markedly hostile manner. After Sarek establishes via mind-meld with Saru that the *Discovery* crew are who they say they are, Cornwell orders the immediate classification of all information regarding the Mirror Universe, before revealing that a divided Klingon Empire now slaughters Federation citizens for sport.

When the Klingons gain a foothold in the Sol System, Michael Burnham learns from Mirror Georgiou that the path to defeating the Klingons goes through Qo'noS. Accordingly, Starfleet hatches a plan to cripple the Klingon homeworld's war machine – one which requires Lieutenant Stamets to terraform a moon and harvest new mycelium spores.

Meanwhile, Saru exhibits incredible empathy for the now Voq-less Tyler, speaking words of comfort and compassion. This stands in marked contrast to Burnham's inability to look at Tyler without seeing Voq, as well as her painful decision to end their relationship.

As Sarek and Georgiou discuss their respective wards, the Vulcan is left with the belief that winning the war will require even more drastic measures. The result? As *Discovery* prepares to jump to Qo'noS, Cornwell announces the mission will be commanded by the newly recovered "Captain" Georgiou.

03

04

05

(Previous spread)

01 Mirror Georgiou unexpectedly finds herself in the Prime Universe.

02 Sarek confers with the former emperor.

AARON HARBERTS
Executive Producer

"I really love Episode 14, 'The War Without, the War Within,' because I thought it was a fantastic way of showing the Federation and Starfleet in really dire straits, and showing the lengths that people are willing to go to – the lengths that war and violence push people to go to.

"We always wanted to make sure that the Federation and Starfleet were redeemed, but that was the darkest tunnel, and I felt that Lisa Randolph, who wrote it, and the director of that episode knocked it out of the park. I thought the break-up scene between Michael and Tyler was really great, and I thought that James

> "Klingons have tasted your blood. Conquer us, or we will never relent."
>
> **L'RELL**

Frain was awesome in this episode as well."

MARY CHIEFFO
L'Rell

"It was not Tyler that was in that relationship [with L'Rell]; it was always Voq. It was just his memories got really screwed up. But that's also my bad! [*Laughs*] The surgeries… But at the same time, from L'Rell's perspective, she did not cross that line, and I think it's very important that we're sensitive to that. It's complex, and it's crazy, and again it's a mythology; I mean, you look at Medea, you look at Antigone, you look at any of Shakespeare's plays: they go to these crazy heights. It's because something deeper in humanity is being explored."

TAMARA DEVERELL
Production Designer

"This year we've had to fix a lot of things up. We had to rebuild the floors of Engineering, and we've been tweaking things – adding a door, and spending as much money as I'm allowed, adding things in corridors and so on… Making some adjustments and improvements to our standing sets as the season continues.

"Originally the mess hall had one entrance, only now it's got two. The mess hall and the quarters were the same set, and last year we were constantly redressing it, and putting walls in, and it was driving everybody crazy, and the set dec department was exhausted. So this year I said, 'Listen, how about we separate them, spend a little money and make a mess hall that's just a mess hall, and a crew quarters that's multipurpose.' So that's one of our tweaks." ⋏

03 A skeptical Sarek.

04 Admiral Cornwell takes command of the *Discovery*.

05 Saru in the captain's chair.

06 Cornwell and Sarek brief the crew on the conflict with the Klingons.

WILL YOU
TAKE MY HAND?

SEASON 1, EPISODE 15

First aired:
February 11, 2018
Teleplay: Gretchen J. Berg
& Aaron Harberts
Story: Akiva Goldsman &
Gretchen J. Berg &
Aaron Harberts
Director: Akiva Goldsman

CAST

Sonequa Martin-Green:
Michael Burnham
Doug Jones:
Commander Saru
Shazad Latif:
Lieutenant Ash Tyler
Anthony Rapp:
Lieutenant Paul Stamets
Mary Wiseman:
Cadet Sylvia Tilly
Michelle Yeoh:
Mirror Emperor
Philippa Georgiou
Mia Kirshner:
Amanda Grayson
Jayne Brook:
Admiral Katrina
Cornwell
Mary Chieffo: L'Rell
James Frain: Sarek
Clint Howard: Orion
Alan van Sprang:
Leland (bonus scene)
Matthew Binkley: Shavo
Emily Coutts:
Lieutenant Keyla Detmer
Clare McConnell: Dennas
Damon Runyan: Ujilli
Sara Mitich: Lieutenant
Commander Airiam
Oyin Oladejo: Lieutenant
Joann Owosekun
Ronnie Rowe Jr.:
Lieutenant R. A. Bryce
Bree Wasylenko: Shava

01

SYNOPSIS

Starfleet's plan to map Klingon military targets as a prelude for a co-ordinated assault on the Empire turns out to be a ploy: former Terran Emperor Georgiou's mapping drone is actually a hydro bomb designed to demolish the planet Qo'noS!

In an effort to avert disaster, Michael Burnham contacts Admiral Cornwell and successfully advocates to reconsider the attack. Though Georgiou releases the bomb into the volcanic chimney, Burnham convinces her not to detonate it. In return, Georgiou receives her freedom, while Burnham persuades L'Rell to use the bomb's trigger to blackmail the Klingon houses into ending the war and uniting under her rule.

With peace restored, Burnham is pardoned and reinstated, her Starfleet insignia presented to her by Sarek. In addition, she and several other *Discovery* crew members are awarded the Starfleet Medal of Honor – including, posthumously, Doctor Hugh Culber – while Paul Stamets and Sylvia Tilly are promoted to, respectively, Lieutenant Commander and Ensign.

As *Discovery* departs Earth, an incoming distress call arrives from Captain Pike... of the *U.S.S. Enterprise*. Meanwhile, on Qo'noS, Georgiou is approached by a disguised Starfleet operative, who has a proposition for her...

> "What's wrong? Are you scared, Number One? Where I'm from, there's a saying: 'Scared Kelpien makes for tough Kelpien.'"
>
> **EMPEROR GEORGIOU TO SARU**

> "We will continue exploring, discovering new worlds, new civilizations. Yes – that is the United Federation of Planets... Yes – that is Starfleet... Yes, that is who we are... And who we will always be."
>
> **MICHAEL BURNHAM**

MARY CHIEFFO
L'Rell

"From my perspective, certainly from where I was in Episode 15, I really didn't think there was any remnant of Voq left, until [Tyler] speaks to me in Klingon. At the end of Episode 12, when I do the surgery – that death wail, that's goodbye Voq, he's no longer there: I choose to make that sacrifice so that Voq doesn't suffer. And so it's such a surprise to suddenly have him still have these memories, even if they're neutered memories.

"It's complicated, too, that it isn't a typical love triangle – that Voq and L'Rell had a legitimate relationship, and Burnham and Tyler had a legitimate relationship, and I think L'Rell is smart enough to get that. I certainly think that they don't walk off into the sunset in that moment; they're not like, 'Oh and everything's fine.' I think that they understand the complexity of it. The possibilities are endless.

"My friend would say to me in college, 'You gotta have the breakdown before the breakthrough,' and I think that L'Rell had that breakdown, and is piecing herself back together, and trying to do the right thing. And ultimately the most important thing in episode 15 for L'Rell was to bring peace, or to understand that this collaboration was more important than any personal grievances."

JASON ZIMMERMAN
Visual Effects Supervisor

"In Episode 15, Akiva, the director, came up with these massive shots where you start in space and you go down all the way into Paris, and then you land and they're talking – it's a huge shot. So we started building; you start building the Earth, and you start building the stuff that's surrounding the Earth, and you build Paris, and you build the ships, and the shuttles, and all that stuff, and you just keep pushing and eventually you get to where it seems like it's fine.

"That shot is probably one of the larger shots we've done in the show, if not *the* largest. The good part of it is that when you receive the script it's a long time before things are gonna be delivered, so if I know that that's gonna stay in the script – and the executive producers are great about saying something will be in the script or won't be – we can actually get going on it right away."

(Previous spread)

01 The proud father with his daughter.

02 Michael Burnham: commander once more.

TAMARA DEVERELL
Production Designer

"It was the last episode, so we kinda used everything we had for the Orion black market sets on Qo'noS. We had a whole season's boatload of bits and pieces of the Klingon ship, because of course we had the Sarcophagus, which blew up; we had a big chunk of the gormagander whale from Episode 7 – which was VFX, but we actually built a chunk of it – so we made a market stall as a gormagander.

"The writers said, 'What can you give us?' So we did a weapons stall, cos we had some weapons; we did different meat stalls – we made things that looked like dim sum but they were moving; a tattoo parlor…

"For the tattoo parlor, the producers wanted something where the couple could go off to. We actually used a closet they were storing set pieces in, cleared it out, and said, 'Okay, this is a tattoo parlor – bring in a bunch of Klingon stuff!' So it was kind of a real group hug to create that world.

"And obviously we had help from the VFX department. Often our process will be to get our concept artists working with me on what the world is – so we drew up Qo'noS, we drew up what the black market was, and then we did it. We do this much and then the VFX department makes it *this big*." ⋀

03 With Saru in command and Sarek along for the ride, *Discovery* embarks on a new mission.

04 The *Discovery* crew receive the Medal of Honor.

05 A proud Admiral Cornwell looks on.

SECRET SECTION

Debuting a month after the *Star Trek: Discovery* Season 1 finale aired, a previously secret bonus scene from the final episode sees the *Discovery* debut of clandestine Federation organization Section 31, in the shape of operative Leland, played by Alan van Sprang. Speaking shortly after the unveiling of that scene, Van Sprang shares his thoughts on his character, and the prospects for Section 31 in Season 2.

01

01 Ex-Emperor Georgiou considers a new career, as she meets Leland of Section 31.

02 Alan van Sprang, pictured at WonderCon 2018, where the secret scene was unveiled.

Star Trek: Discovery Companion:
What do you know about Section 31?
Alan van Sprang: Section 31 is basically an intelligence agency that doesn't exist. Everyone that knows *Star Trek* knows who Section 31 is, and so apparently I'm part of that!

What are you most excited about, heading into Season 2 of *Star Trek: Discovery?*
The fact that it's a mystery to me as well.

I came in to the final [episode of the] season… Aaron [Harberts] and Gretchen [J. Berg] approached me last year – they knew who I was and wanted me to be part of the show – and being part of this new show is really exciting.

Have you been sworn to secrecy about Season 2?
It's not really that I can't say anything about it, but, I honestly feel like I know nothing about it! I really don't. I did the

last [scene] of Episode 15, that's what you saw. I trust Aaron and Gretchen.

It's a mystery, which I really enjoy and I really appreciate. And they're great writers, and I think the show is kick-ass. I watched the entire first season. I'm a big *Star Trek* fan. I was a big *Next Generation* fan but this is second to that, to me. And then the original [series] as well. But this one I really, really like.

It was interesting, because with Jason Isaacs' character, some people

"WILL YOU TAKE MY HAND?"
BONUS SCENE

Some time after being granted her freedom by the Federation, the Mirror Universe Philippa Georgiou is still on Qo'noS, now running a salacious cabaret in the Orion black market. There, she is approached by Leland, a mysterious individual whose disguise as a Trill Georgiou easily sees through. Pointing out that running a cabaret isn't the best use of Georgiou's skills, Leland notes that though the war with the Klingons is over, it's still a dangerous universe, and that peace comes with a moral cost. When Georgiou counters that Leland doesn't sound like Starfleet, he responds that he's not: his organization is far more resourceful, and believes Georgiou could be a valuable asset. Giving Georgiou a black Starfleet insignia, Leland departs, declaring: "Welcome to Section 31."

03

actually thought that he might be part of Section 31, and that *Discovery* was a part of that. That's just what I read today, as I was investigating my own character…

Did you watch any previous appearances of Section 31 for research – episodes of *Star Trek: Deep Space Nine*, for example?
Yeah, that's what I did, I watched all of *Deep Space Nine*, so I found out [info] through [Section 31 operative Luther Sloan] and [Doctor Bashir] from that show, and their relationship and what they were doing. I watched those episodes, and I think this is even more mysterious than that, even though that was great.

03 Alan van Sprang as Leland – in Trill disguise – in the Season 1 finale, "Will You Take My Hand?"

04 Section 31 operative Luther Sloan with Captain Sisko in *Star Trek: Deep Space Nine*'s "Inquisition."

04

What other research have you had a chance to do?
There are novels based on Section 31, so I'm just starting to read those. My last show that I did, *Shadowhunters: The Mortal Instruments*, there are so many books on that, so I was reading those and that was amazing, but Section 31 I'm really interested in.

Whatever I've researched I think will be helpful for all of us, because it's a really interesting part of *Star Trek*, having this intelligence agency.

How do you think you'll approach the performance of Leland, in

comparison to your previous genre roles?
Just before *Shadowhunters* I did a series called *Reign*, and it was just sort of evil characters. And so I approached [the new role] not in the same way. I always approach characters in a different way. I did a Gene Roddenberry series 20 years ago, *Earth: Final Conflict*, and I played an Atavus alien creature in that for a season, but with this, I'm not going about it as a bad guy. What I'm getting from the creators, is that I'm more of an inspiration to certain characters – at least that's what I'm assuming I'm gonna portray – an

05 Section 31 agent Harris in *Star Trek: Enterprise*'s "Affliction."

06 The duplicitous Sloan in *Deep Space Nine*'s "Inter Arma Enim Silent Leges."

inspiration to these people, making them go from evil to not. It's probably the first time in a long time I'm just gonna be, I think, a mysterious good guy. Even though in the clip, I'm in disguise… He's gonna be, hopefully, a cool enough character… He's mysterious, but I think the surprise there will be that he inspires a lot of the people in the show.

Which characters from previous *Star Trek* series could you see Leland trying to recruit?
Q. [*Laughs*] He was my favorite character. ⋀

SECTION 31
FURTHER VIEWING

STAR TREK: DEEP SPACE NINE

"Inquisition"
(Season 6, Episode 18)
Doctor Bashir is accused of being a Dominion spy by Luther Sloan – who then attempts to recruit him.

"Inter Arma Enim Silent Leges"
(Season 7, Episode 16)
Sloan involves Bashir in a Section 31 scheme to keep the Romulans allied with the Federation.

"Extreme Measures"
(Season 7, Episode 23)
In search of a cure to the disease that is killing Odo, Bashir lures Sloan to Deep Space 9.

STAR TREK: ENTERPRISE

"Affliction"/"Divergence"
(Season 4, Episodes 15–16)
Former Section 31 operative Lieutenant Malcolm Reed's loyalties to his current *Enterprise* crewmates are sorely tested.

"Demons"/"Terra Prime"
(Season 4, Episodes 20–21)
Section 31 operative Harris provides intelligence to the *Enterprise* crew on the terrorist group Terra Prime.

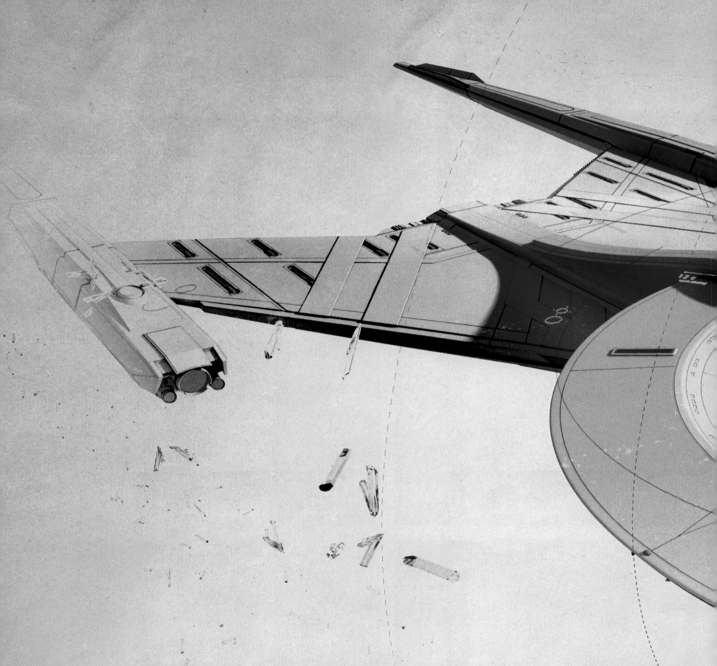

STAR TREK™
DISCOVERY

OTHER GREAT TIE-IN COMPANIONS FROM TITAN
ON SALE NOW!

Star Trek: The Movies
ISBN 9781785855924

Fifty Years of Star Trek
ISBN 9781785855931

**Star Trek – A Next
Generation Companion**
ISBN 9781785855948

**Star Trek Discovery
Collector's Edition**
ISBN 9781785861581

**Star Wars: Lords of
the Sith**
ISBN 9781785851919

**Star Wars:
Heroes of the Force**
ISBN 9781785851926

**The Best of Star Wars
Insider Volume 1**
ISBN 9781785851162

**The Best of Star Wars
Insider Volume 2**
ISBN 9781785851179

**The Best of Star Wars
Insider Volume 3**
ISBN 9781785851896

**The Best of Star Wars
Insider Volume 4**
ISBN 9781785851902

**Star Wars:
Icons Of The Galaxy**
ISBN 9781785851933

**Star Wars: The Last Jedi
The Official Collector's Edition**
ISBN 9781785862113

**Star Wars: The Last Jedi
The Official Movie Companion**
ISBN 9781785863004

**Solo: A Star Wars Story
The Official Movie Companion**
ISBN 9781785863011

**Thor Ragnarok
Movie Special**
ISBN 9781785866371

**Black Panther
Movie Special**
ISBN 9781785866531

**Ant-Man and the Wasp
Movie Special**
ISBN 9781785868092

**Avengers: Infinity War
Movie Special**
ISBN 9781785868054

TITANCOMICS
For more information visit www.titan-comics.com